S0-BNY-067

# *Fishing Moments of Truth*

# Fishing Moments of Truth

Edited by
Eric Peper
Jim Rikhoff
Drawings by Milton C. Weiler

WINCHESTER PRESS

Library of Congress Catalog Card Number: 73-78820
ISBN 0-87691-112-2 (regular edition)
ISBN 0-87691-123-8 (limited edition)

Published by Winchester Press
460 Park Avenue, New York 10022

Printed in the United States of America

For

*Larry Koller*

*Jack Randolph*

*John Alden Knight*

*Richard Alden Knight*

and

*Joe Brooks*

Fine fishermen and writers all—
they should have been in this book.

## Contents

# *Testament of a Fisherman*

ROBERT TRAVER

*I fish because I love to; because I love the environs where trout are found, which are invariably beautiful, and I hate the environs where crowds of people are found, which are invariably ugly; because of all the television commercials, cocktail parties, and assorted social posturing I thus escape; because in a world where most men seem to spend their lives doing things they hate, my fishing is at once an endless source of delight and an act of small rebellion; because trout do not lie or cheat and cannot be bought or bribed or impressed by power, but respond only to quietude and humility and endless patience; because I suspect that men are going along this way for the last time, and I for one don't want to waste the trip; because mercifully there are no telephones on trout waters; because only in the woods can I find solitude without loneliness; because bourbon out of an old tin cup always tastes better out there; because maybe one day I will catch a mermaid; and, finally, not because I regard fishing as being so terribly important but because I suspect that so many of the other concerns of men are equally unimportant—and not nearly so much fun.*

---

# *Foreword*

It was the Spanish, of course, who conceived the idea of a "moment of truth" as a dramatized description of the elegant crisis of the bullfight. Later, Hemingway communicated that peculiar Spanish institution to North Americans when he wrote *Death in the Afternoon,* and "moment of truth" has enjoyed a secure niche in English literature and language ever since. Hemingway would appreciate the significance of using the phrase in the title of this collection of the very personal experiences of a group of dedicated anglers, because he was an enthusiastic hunter and fisherman himself.

There is no Hemingway fishing story in this book, however—because every piece is an original, written for this collection, with the exception of Robert Traver's exceptional "Testament to a Fisherman," which occupies a justified position in the front of the book before the main body of stories. Traver's piece deserves to be reprinted at least every year or two. A few of the other stories will appear in magazines—some perhaps before this book is published—but the majority of stories are seeing print for the first and maybe the last time.

There is a good reason why this is a one-time, better-read-it-while-you-can collection. Most of the stories included in this anthology were written for the book and not a magazine, and as such—let's face it—many simply would never reach the light of day in magazine format. Quite simply, we have tried to give the author-sportsman a freedom seldom given in magazine assignments. The reader will find a paucity of "Me and Joe Caught the Monster Bass" stories in this volume. The avid home gadgeteer will be disappointed if he expects some secret method to improve his favorite widget spinning reel. What he will find is something quite again different—stories that reflect the almost primeval urge men feel and the continued satisfaction they enjoy in pursuit of fish, large and small, in salt and fresh water.

In short, I suppose our title *Fishing Moments of Truth* fairly well indicates the direction we sought in this volume. We feel that every fisherman—rich or poor, young or old, and of whatever nationality—has at least one experience that crystallizes that particular moment that makes fishing for him. It may be a frustrating near miss, a poignant break-off, a hilarious fiasco, a sad twilight reward, an early-morning contest. As one can see, fishing can be many things to many men, but its effects would be much the same—a fanatical adherence to the fishing mystique.

Eric Peper and I considered a very large number of possible contributors that rapidly diminished as we matched them against the rather stringent criteria for inclusion. We feel that the writers selected—Lee Wulff, Ernest Schwiebert, Dana Lamb, Roderick Haig-Brown, Charles Ritz, Art Flick, Charles Fox, Nick Lyons, Arnold Gingrich, Ed Zern, Steve Raymond, Angus Cameron, Ed Koch, Pat Smith, Lamar Underwood, Pete Hidy, Homer Circle, Jack Samson, Nelson Bryant, Grits Gresham, Charles Waterman and the aforementioned Robert Traver (John Voelker, that is)—more than justify our efforts and our hopes. Our wish is that those that pick up this book will find a few moments of truth and many hours of pleasure.

*Jim Rikhoff*
*Speakeasy Hill*
*High Bridge, New Jersey*

*May 30, 1973*

# Fishing Moments of Truth

# On the Divide

NICK LYONS

## I

For three days we fished the lake without a strike. We rose each morning at four, dressed quickly by the bald light of the bulb in the kitchen of the cabin, and then carried our rods and tackle bags silently through the darkness, down the hill to the aluminum boat.

The motor started only once on the first pull of the cord. Neither of us was adept at motors, and we wore our hands raw with frantic tugging. Once, far out on the lake, when the winds came rushing along the Continental Divide in which the lake was set like a glittering blue jewel, we pulled anchor, could not start the motor, and drifted half across the lake before another fisherman came after us. I tried to row, busted an oar, and ripped more skin off the palms of my hands.

On the fourth morning the alarm was only a dull ringing far back in my head. The ringing stopped, and then the memory of it woke me. I went into his room to wake him, but he only turned and arched up his body like a cat stretching. "I can't . . ." he said. "I can't make it today."



I dressed and gathered up my fly rod and the little teardrop net I always wore fastened to my vest, and the burlap creel in which I carried my reels and flies. I went down to the lake alone, which is how I usually fished anyway. It was better alone, I thought. Then you didn't have to worry if the other person was enjoying himself, whether he would catch the fish you had dreamed of all winter, whether he would see your poor casts. Sometimes with the experts I'd seen fishing turn to fierce competition.

The boy had stopped casting that last afternoon. I had asked him why, and he had answered curtly, "What's the use?"

"They're here," I told him. "Big ones. Up to four, five, even ten pounds."

"Sure," he said.

"They are. Dave told me he hooked a tremendous trout here last September. He had it on for nearly an hour. He said it was actually—"

"—towing his boat. You've told me that. In Cincinnati, Sioux City, Cody, and—"

"Guess I did," I said. "But they're here. I'll swear to it."

"Then why haven't we caught any?" he asked.

"Maybe they haven't come into the channel yet; maybe we haven't found the right fly or lure; maybe—"

"—maybe they're not here," he said. "Maybe they were here sixteen years ago when you say you caught all those monsters."

"Yes, they were here," I said quietly. "I killed a great number of trout when I came to the lake sixteen years ago."

"You said your arms were tired from catching so many."

"They were."

"You said *my* arms would be tired."

I had looked out across the lake, at the surrounding sagebrush flat with its pastures and fences and scattered trees, and at the mountains of the Continental Divide that rimmed the lake, some still snowcapped though it was midsummer. We had fished seven hours without a strike, and the sun was now high and hot.

"Can't we go back," he said, "or run the boat around the lake a couple of times? I like to run the kicker."

The word sounded strange on his tongue. It was a new word and fit him like a ready-made suit. We had not been in a boat together before, and I was pleased that he enjoyed running the kicker.

"I'd like to fish," I said.

"For how long?" he asked, turning from me and fingering the rubber covering on the handle of the kicker, turning it slightly several times without pulling the cord.

"We came a long way to fish this lake," I said. "More than two thousand miles. I think we'll get some trout if we'll . . . only . . . be patient enough."

"Well, I'm tired."

And then he'd put the rod in the bottom of the aluminum boat carelessly, and tucked his head down into his mackinaw jacket though the sun was high and hot. I'd fished for another half hour and had not caught a thing.

On the fourth morning the air was wet and cold. There was a thin drizzle, and I rolled down the rim of the expensive khaki hat I'd bought in the city a week before the trip and lifted the collar of my old hunting coat. This time I pressed the rubber bulb near the gasoline can four or five times sharply before I pulled the cord, pumping it until it grew hard. The motor started on the first pull, and I backed out of the dock and out into the springs.

There were a few lights, and the moon still gave enough light to see by. I eased the boat under the wire that stretched across the springs into which the fish came when the weather warmed and headed out into the channel. When I was parallel to the great clump of willows on shore, I turned left and cut my speed, running the boat slowly until I thought I was in the deepest part of the channel. "Glory Hole" the spot was called, and I had only learned of it the day before from the manager of the cabins. I had fished in the springs the first time I'd come to the lake; there had been thousands of trout in the springs then, and there had been no need to fish from a boat. I had caught and killed a great number of them one night sixteen years earlier. It was better that the springs were closed, but I had hoped the boy could fish in them and catch some of the huge trout I had caught. One fish would be enough, if it was the right fish.

I let down the large tin can filled with cement. The anchor chain felt cold and harsh against my torn hands. The barest light was breaking behind the mountains to the east; it came first from the "V" of the mountains, where two pyramids crossed, and then the whole sky to the east grew lighter.

I tied on a long brown leech, with a brown marabou tail, wet it in my mouth, and then began to strip line from my new Princess reel. Soon I had a good length of line working back and forward, and then I laid it out as far as I could and dropped the rod tip to the surface of the water as I'd seen several men do the day before. In a minute or so I began the methodical short-strips retrieve, slowly bringing the fly back through the black waters. It was a rhythmic process and not at all like the dry-fly fishing I had always done in the East. Everything was feel. I had fished the lake with spinning lures that summer after my release from the Army. I had come alone and stayed for four days that had stayed pristine these past sixteen years. But now, with flies, I had not been able to induce a strike. Five, six times I cast, and each time waited and then brought the fly back slowly—strip, strip, strip, pause; strip, strip, strip.

It was good, I thought, that the boy had not come out with me. The air grew colder as the mists formed on the lake, and the drizzle grew into a light rain. My hands were already numb, and no one else had yet come onto the lake. I heard unseen sheep baying in one of the meadows.

I enjoyed being on the lake alone, and I enjoyed casting the long line and then bringing back the fly with that slow, methodical retrieve. The years had been long and crowded and hard, and I had watched some of my dreams die and I had not been home enough—not nearly enough—and I had thought all winter and all spring, for several years, of coming back to this lake, where I had once made such a large catch. I wanted to catch some of the big trout very much, on flies. You progressed from worms to lures to flies, and then flies made all the difference. I had wanted the boy to catch some of the big trout, it didn't matter how.

The tip of my rod jerked down sharply. I raised it and felt the heavy throbbing as the line arched out and away. It was a good fish.

The fish moved off to the left and I reeled in the loose line so I could fight him from the reel. Twice he broke water but did not jump. Cutthroat, I thought. I knew that the cutthroat broke water but that the brooks in this lake usually did not. There were hybrids in the lake, too, crosses between the rainbow and the cutthroat, but they would not often jump either.

The fish was not as large as I'd pictured him, and I soon had him alongside and into my little stream net. He was about two pounds. Because we wouldn't be eating the fish, I took the hook out and turned out the net. In the net the fish was bright red. Now as I watched he wavered slowly, his back spotted and the red no longer visible, then darted down and out of sight.

I cast out immediately and after waiting for the fly to sink, began the slow retrieve again. Again the rod tip shot down, and I took another cutthroat about the same size. When I had turned this one out of the net, I sat down on the green boat-cushion and took out a cigar. I breathed deeply several times, lit my cigar, and looked over toward the east. It was still raining lightly, and the sun had not yet broken. Christ, it was good to be out on this lake alone, after all the years, after all the changes.

Several other boats were anchored in the channel now, and a man in one of them was fast to a good fish.

"On the leech?" the other man called out.

"Yep. Brown and long, with marabou."

I waited another ten minutes while the fish was brought to the boat. As the man finally lifted it high with his huge boat net, I could see it was a gorgeous male brookie.

The other man had a fish on now, too. The trout had come into the hole. There might be hundreds of them, all staging into the channel that led to the springs.

I cast again, and again took a fine trout. I was in the right spot, in the right hole, and there were many fish, and I had the right fly.

I took two more, about three pounds each, and then, after three fruitless casts, hooked a fish I could not stop. I felt when he took that he was heavy. He did not rush like the others, angling to one side while the line angled up and up. This fish moved straight away from the boat—slowly and steadily; *thump—thump—thump.* Soon he had all my stripping line out, and he began to take line off the reel with the same slow, confident power.

And then he stopped.

I lifted the rod tip to be sure he was still there. There was a heavy weight, but I felt no movement. Perhaps he's sulking, I thought. I lifted the rod again and felt the same dead weight. For several minutes I stood, putting constant pressure on the line but not enough to break it. My chest was beating heavily; my right hand shook.

"In the weeds?" one of the men asked.

"Don't know. Something's still down there. I can feel something."

"Better pull the line with your hand," the man said. "If he's still on, you'll feel him."

I did so and only felt the dead weight.

I gave the line a few more steady pulls, then drew it tight and gave it a sharp tug. When I got the line in, I saw some weeds still attached to it. The fish had wound himself around and around until he was able to break off; I'd never felt the break.

"Tough luck," one of the men called. "Must have been a big brookie—or maybe a hybrid."

"I couldn't turn him," I said.

"One of the big hybrids, probably. Eight, maybe ten pounds. Larger even."

I took a deep breath and sat down. My hands were still shaking, so I pressed them against my knees. Then I went into my fly box and fumbled for another of the leeches I'd been given by a neighbor the day before. I breathed deeply again, thought of the boy, and decided to head back to the cabin.

"You really took five and lost a big one?" the boy said as we sat at the linoleum-topped table. His eyes were wide, and his bushy black hair, dried by the sun, stood up wildly. He was rested, and I could tell he was excited as he wolfed down a doughnut we'd bought in town the night before. "Five? And they were about three pounds? Why didn't you keep them? I'd have kept them. Every one of them."

"All the men were getting good fish," I said.

"Why didn't you wake me?"

"I tried to, old man, but you wouldn't be woke."

"Want to go back out? Do you think I can get a couple? *Everyone was getting them?* How many fish did you actually see caught?"

"Whenever you're ready we'll go back out," I said, smiling.

"You're sure I can get some? They're in the channel, like the manager said they'd be this week?"

"Let's find out," I said.

The lake was crowded now. As I moved the boat out of the springs and into the channel, I could see at once that the Glory Hole now had eight or ten boats anchored in or near it. The sun had burned off the mist, and the rain had stopped. It was late morning, and I could see down into the water, right to the bottom in the areas that didn't have weeds. It was a shallow lake and not particularly clear, and in the summer the weeds grew thick and high. I saw several large fish swimming slowly along the bottom and cut the motor. The boy looked over the side as we circled back, and he saw them too. They were large brook trout—four or five pounds apiece.

"Did you see them, Dad?" he asked. "Did you see the *size* of them?"

"I saw."

"Shall we fish here?"

"Let's head further out," I said. "Near where I got them this morning."

We headed out toward the hole, but several boats were anchored where I had been. I did not want to fish too close to them. I wished there were no other boats on the lake.

Finally, we cut the motor at the edge of the weeds where the hole abruptly ended. I told the boy to cast toward the other boats. His rod was rigged, and he began to cast before I'd fully lowered the anchor chain. He drew the lure back quickly, with the rod tip held high and steady. He made four casts this way; I watched him while I tied on another leech and checked my leader for frays.

"Put the rod tip down and bring the lure back in short jerks," I said. "You're bringing it back too fast."

"Like this?" he asked, and lowered the rod and brought the lure back even faster, still without the short jerks that had worked so well for me sixteen years earlier.

"No, no," I said. "Slower. Slower."

One of the men in my morning spot had hooked another fish on a fly rod, and he fought it noisily with Texas howls. The boy looked over and began to reel his lure in fast again.

In a few minutes another man had a fish on his fly rod, and then another rod bent in that high curving arc, too. I began to cast now, from the bow of our boat, and on the third cast hooked a solid cutthroat.

"This spinning rod is no good," the boy said.

"It will catch more and bigger fish than a fly," I told him.

"That's what you said while we were driving here. All the way across the country you told me I'd have no trouble catching fish with a spinning rod. I haven't gotten a thing. Not a strike."

I put my rod down and took his spinning rod. It was a strange weapon in my hands. I had not used one in many years. I had stopped using a spinning rod after I'd fished this lake the last time and had gone through a long apprenticeship learning the magic of a fly rod. I had caught nothing for a long time, and then suddenly the line no longer whipped down on the water behind me, and the fly no longer slapped down on the water, and my distance grew from twenty to forty and then maybe sixty-five feet.

I flicked the metal lure far out into the hole and let it sink, and then brought it back in short, sharp jerks. I cast three or four more times, drew the lure back with those slow, sharp jerks, and then handed the rod to the boy. He cast again and then again. He imparted a better motion to the lure now, but he still caught no fish. The other men took three more fish on their fly rods.

I cast again and then again. On the fourth cast I hooked another cutthroat. He splashed at the surface several times and then came in without difficulty.

"I can't get a thing," the boy said. "I'm just no good at it. I'll never catch anything."

"You will. I'm sure you will."

"You've been saying that."

"Try a few more casts," I coached.

"Why?"

"You can't catch anything if you don't cast."

"And I can't catch anything if I do cast."

The sun was bright and hot now, and many of the boats were beginning to head back to the dock. I pulled the anchor and headed closer to the center of the hole.

But when we'd anchored in the new spot and he'd cast four or five more times, he gave it up and sat down.

"How long are we going to stay here?" he asked.

"We can go back now," I said. "I only wanted you to get a couple of fish."

"I haven't caught any," he said.

"I know," I said.

"Look, Dad," he said. "I like fishing, I really do. And I like being out here with you. But I can't catch anything on this spinning rod. Maybe if I knew how to use a fly rod it would be different. But I don't. And I don't have the same kind of patience you have. I like fishing, but I don't like not catching anything. You don't care. You really don't. But I do. And I'm not going to get any. Not today. Not tomorrow. Not any day this week. I know I won't."

"Well," I said, scratching my head, "why don't you try twenty more casts, and if you don't get one we'll head back to the cabin and maybe visit Virginia City or the Park this afternoon." Perhaps we should head back at once, I thought. I had enjoyed being on the lake alone at daybreak—catching some fish, losing the big fish. Perhaps it had been a mistake to come back to this lake with the boy. He would have enjoyed the beach more, and I wouldn't have wanted to fish so much. I never seemed to fish enough, but it mattered much less when there were no trout nearby.

The boy began casting and counting, bringing in the lure much too fast. Thirteen, fourteen, fifteen. Nothing. Sixteen. Nothing.

On the seventeenth cast the little glass rod jerked down in a sharp arc. A good fish. A very good fish.

"Good grief!" he shouted. "Can't hold him!"

"Let him have line," I shouted back. "Don't force him. Keep your rod tip high. It's a good fish, a *very* good fish."

The fish moved steadily from the boat. I could tell by the way the line throbbed slowly that it was a substantial fish, a brookie I thought.

The boy lowered the rod tip and I leaned over to lift it up. The boat swayed and I never reached the rod, but the boy smiled broadly and raised the rod so that the full force of the bend could work against the fish.

Don't lose it. For God's sake don't lose it, I thought.

"He's still taking line, Dad. I can't stop him."

"He'll turn," I said. "He's got to turn in a minute or two. Don't force him. Don't let him get into the weeds, but don't force him. *Don't drop that rod tip!*"

The line went slack.

"No. No!" I said.

"Have I lost him? No. I *can't* have lost him."

"Reel quickly," I said. "Maybe he's turned. Maybe he's still there."

"He's there," the boy shouted. "I can feel him. Good grief, he's big. Can you see him yet? I won't lose him now."

I looked over where the line entered the water. I strained to see the fish but could not. It had to be a big brookie.

Now the fish was angling off to the left. He might go completely around the boat. As the line came toward me, I lifted it and let it pass over my head. For a second I could feel the big fish throbbing at the other end of the line. The fish came around the front of the boat, and the boy fought him on the other side.

We both saw him at the same time. A huge male brookie. We saw him twisting and shaking ten feet below the surface, the silver lure snug in the corner of his mouth.

"He's huge. It's the biggest brookie I've ever seen."

"I'm not going to lose him," the boy said. "I can't lose him now."

"You won't lose him. He's well hooked. He's too high and too tired to get into the weeds. You've got him beat, son. I'll get the net." I looked under the seat and came up with the little teardrop stream net.

"He'll never fit," the boy said. "He'll *never* fit in that—*whooooa.* He's taking line again. He's going around the other side of the boat now."

The fish was close to the boat but not yet beaten. He went deep and around the corner of the boat. I watched for the line to angle out, on the other side of the boat. It never did.

"The anchor chain!" I shouted. "Don't let him get in the anchor chain."

"I can't feel him," said the boy. "The line's on something, but I can't feel the fish fighting any more."

I scurried the length of the boat, bent under the rod, and then lowered myself where the anchor chain entered the water. At first I could see nothing, but then I saw it. The huge brook trout was still on the line. I could see him five feet down, the silver lure still in the corner of his mouth. He was circling slowly around the anchor chain, and I could see that the line was already wound six or seven times around the links. It would not come free. Not ever.

"Is it there?" the boy called. "Is it still there?"

"You're going to lose him, son. He's in the anchor chain. There's no way I can get it free."

"Oh, no, *no,*" he said.

I put my nose down to the surface of the water. The fish had gone around the chain twice more, and his distance from the chain was growing smaller. He kept circling, slowly, every now and then jerking his head back against the tug of the line.

"I can't lose him! I can't," the boy said.

"There's nothing to be done. If I lift the chain, he'll break off; if I leave him, he'll pull out in another couple of turns."

"What about the net?"

"Don't think I can reach him."

"Try, Dad. *Please* try. I can't lose this fish. Not this one."

I took the little stream net and dipped it far down. The cold water stung my raw hands, and the net came short by more than a foot. The fish made a lunge, and I was sure it would break free.

"Get him?"

"Nope. Too far down. Can't reach him."

"Maybe someone with one of the boat nets . . ." But he stopped. The other boats were gone from the lake; we had the Glory Hole to ourselves.

The fish went around the rope again. There was only a foot and a half between him and the chain now. The big brookie was tired. He was half on his side.

I took the boy's arm and pulled him down to where I knelt. It didn't matter if he let the line go slack now. Together we pushed our faces close to the surface of the water and peered down. In the liquid below us, we looked through the reflections of our faces, side by side, overlapping and rippled, and we saw the huge fish.

I reached again, pressing the net down through the water as carefully as I could, trying hard not to frighten the fish again. My arm was in up to my shoulder, and I felt the cold lake water slosh onto my chest. The fish came a little higher this time. I could almost touch it with the end of the net—and I saw clearly now that even if I could get near enough to it, the fish was far too big for the little net, and the lure was almost torn out. There was no chance.

"You'll never get him, Dad," the boy said.

He was holding onto my shoulder now with his left arm and looking constantly through our reflections at the shadow that was his fish.

"It's lost," I whispered.

And then the fish floated up five or six inches. I pressed the net toward its head, felt cold water on my face, saw the head of the huge fish go into the net, saw the line break behind the lure, and lifted madly.

A year has passed, and the etching remains, as if fixed by acid in steelplate: our faces in the water, merged; the tremendous circling trout; the fish half in and half out of that tiny teardrop net; and then the two of us, side by side in the bottom of that aluminum boat, our raw hands clutching a thing bright silver-gray and mottled, and laughing as if we were four days drunk.

# The Patriarch

STEVE RAYMOND



The spring appeared as a round pool of clear water, oozing slowly from beneath the roots of the big pine that towered over it. The water was cold and pure after having been filtered through countless layers of lava from the point where it had first fallen as snow on the upper slopes.

In July, when the runoff still was near its height, the pool spilled over with a forceful current and gave birth to a noisy little stream. The stream sprawled and spilled its way down the slope and through a meadow, then down another slope. The soft earth along its banks held the tracks of many deer that had come to drink from the stream, and occasionally, between the rains, a set of solitary bear tracks also would remain.

In its lower reaches the little stream flowed through a thick grove of lodgepole pines, the forest floor matted thick with their cast-off needles. Scrub alder grew among the pines along with ferns and scattered spruce, and the shade along the stream was deep and lasting. In its last quarter mile before it entered the lake, the stream chuckled over a bed of rich gravel, the stones worn smooth by the spring freshets, polished slate and amber, brown and white. It was here that the Trout was born.

The day of its emergence was warm, and sunlight dappled the water through the moving foliage above it. Little mayflies were hatching, riding down the diverging currents to dry their wings, and here and there an awkward yellow stonefly fluttered overhead. Already the stream was populated with alevins that had come out in an earlier emergence, and beneath the undercut grassy banks lurked the larger yearling fish that had not answered the migratory call in their first year of life.

With all this life and movement at hand, the arrival of another newcomer was not noticed. In one moment the tiny Trout lived in the darkness it had known throughout its short life, and in the next it suddenly was bathed in a flood of brilliance as it answered the instinctive urge to swim upward through the gravel creases. The current found it quickly, caught it, turned it sideways and swept it down until the fish turned back against it and swam to sanctuary behind the shelter of a larger rock, where it joined three other alevins already resting there.

There the four of them remained, for days and weeks, though time was not known to them. They learned to feed, moving awkwardly at first, then with greater efficiency to capture the microscopic bits of life, the tiny insect larvae and other food the current brought to them. Tiny scales appeared on their bodies for the first time and caught the sunlight in quicksilver flashes when they turned.

They also learned the presence of danger, and one paid with his life when a diving kingfisher suddenly crashed through the surface in a splintering explosion of light and caught the little fish in its long, pointed beak. The other trout quickly scattered in a frantic search for concealment, and many hours passed before—one by one—the surviving three moved cautiously back to their station behind the sheltering stone. From that moment they responded with instant flight to each sudden movement, each fleeting shadow.

July passed, and the warm dog days of August came. The water oozing from the spring was less now, and the sun warmed it as it ran slowly through the open meadow. The three fish still resting behind the stone somehow sensed the lower water, the stronger light, the warming temperature, and they grew even more wary in their feeding, as did those other fish around them. They grew more restless, too, and now and then one would edge away from the rock to the streambank and drop down with the current several feet below the rock, then slowly return as if reluctant to do so.

The sun rose one morning, and the little Trout found itself alone behind the rock. Its companions had slipped away during the night, joining a school of downstream fry that the remaining Trout had dimly sensed passing in the darkness. Something within the Trout was stirring, a strange nervousness, and it spent that day and the next shifting and turning restlessly behind the rock, dropping down and moving back, edging toward the cutbank only to return eventually to its familiar station.

Finally, in the close heat of an August night while heat lightning played in silent, shifting waves along the horizon, the Trout began its journey. Another school of fry was passing downstream, their small, dark shapes fleetingly visible as they moved together in silent communion. The Trout left the shelter of its familiar stone and joined the ranks of the other fry, feeling a sense of safety in their numbers and a sudden, exhilarating freedom as he started down the stream to an unknown destination.

Slowly the school made its way downstream in the warm, gentle current, pressing closely against the banks, joined now and then by other fry, singly or in twos and threes. It collided with another school, mixed and split apart into three schools, then four, merging and mingling until again there were only two. The schools felt their way downstream in darkness, faltering, turning and circling like an uncertain flight of geese; resting in the small pools, riding quickly down the shallow rapids, scattering in sudden, false fear, then joining up again.

The eastern sky slowly turned from total darkness to a deep

purple, then faded to the color of a robin's egg as the horizon rushed toward the sun. The dull, early light touched the rippling water and the schools of migrating fry paused and waited in a pair of tiny pools. Then the sun's upper rim crested the brow of a distant ridge and threw yellow brilliance and long tree shadows across the stream, and the fry sank quickly to the bottom, waiting, nearly motionless in the gravel, impatient for the day to pass.

The kingfishers remained at work throughout the day, and some of the less wary fish were taken. And now and then a dead or dying fish would be swept by in the current, fry that had been injured by predators or had failed the stern test of competition with their fellows for the meager food of the stream. The number of surviving fry now clustered in the gravel was much less than the number that had first emerged, and in the days to come the number would grow smaller still.

The day passed slowly for the waiting fish, anxious now to resume their journey, and they shifted back and forth nervously, touching sides in the crowded little pools. In the afternoon a great bank of tall, ugly thunderheads drifted in from the west and changed the day from one of brilliant light to one of somber gray. Without waiting for final darkness, some of the more bold and venturesome fry slipped away and started downstream.

But then a quick little wind sprang up, rattling the alder leaves along the stream, and the pinetops bowed unanimously toward the east. From the great, dark bulwark of clouds there came a sudden spit of blue light followed by an instant crack of thunder, and the concussion shook the water and slammed against the tiny silver sides of the fry. More lightning followed, and a heavy rain swept into the forest with a dull, hollow roar, the great drops sizzling as they struck the stream.

It grew prematurely dark, but the fry remained in their hiding places. The few who had resumed their downstream trip soon sought out new sanctuaries of their own. Long into the night the storm raged, the rain coming in heavy squalls on the foot of the wind, the lightning creating split-second, twisted shadows in the woods, the thunder rumbling and trembling the earth as if it came from within it. And all this time the fry held steady, swaying in the concussion of the thunder, waiting for the storm to pass.

The sunrise found only a few shreds of darkened cloud as

the last vestige of the storm. The dry forest had eagerly absorbed the rain, and there was only the slightest surge to the current of the stream. The pines glinted with all the colors of the spectrum as the early sunlight caught the droplets still clinging to them, and the air was clean and fresh after the storm had washed it. High on a distant ridge curled a dirty-brown trail of smoke from a forest fire set by the lightning. As the sun reached down again and touched the stream, the fry still waited impatiently.

They waited through the long, bright day, and as soon as the light was off the water they began again their halting descent. By the first, faint gleam of dawn they were near the lake, and a few of the bolder fish pressed on, somehow sensing that their destination was close. The Trout was among them, and as the first flash of sun lit the day it passed out over the rock and rubble at the mouth of the stream and into the still, clear water of the lake.

Here the Trout found cover in the weeds that grew in the shallows and food in the awkward shrimp that swam among the weeds, and in the large, rich larvae and nymphs of the aquatic insects that seemed to be everywhere. He lived in the shallows that first fall until the lake froze in the winter, and again through the following spring and summer, growing quickly as he sought the natural forage of the lake with ever growing efficiency. He was joined by many of his fellows, and together they learned that their new abundance brought with it new dangers in the shape of plunging ospreys and diving ducks and loons. When the Trout began its second summer in the lake, only one of a hundred of its generation still survived, and these survived because they were the strongest and the quickest of all the fry that had swum up through the gravel of the tributary stream.

The Trout grew larger and left its familiar forage grounds in the shallows to move into deeper water, still feeding on shrimp and snails and insects, but now entering the shallows only in the darkness of the evening when it felt secure from whatever danger might be present there. Other fish fell victim to anglers' lures, but the Trout was not deceived and still ranged free, never having felt the pull of a hook or the sudden restraint from an angler's line.

Two more years passed, two seasons of rich feeding, until the Trout grew to become a fish of rare size and strength. Others of its brood were drawn back to the little stream to spawn, but the Trout remained clean and bright, untouched by the changes that had gone on within the bodies of the others. Unbeknownst to it, the same changes were beginning in it as the fall of its fifth year in the lake approached, but it would not feel the full effects of them until the following spring. It rested by day in the shade of the deep, fed cautiously and well on the hatches that came in the evening and grew ever stronger, a creature born of the wild, as free as the wind.

All through the night the rain had drummed steadily on the cabin roof, and it did not cease with morning. Burning wood cracked loudly in the old stove, and its heat seeped slowly out to burn away the chill. Soon the sizzle and scent of frying bacon was added to the crackle of the fire.

I watched the strange course of the rain on the old glass windowpane. The droplets spattered onto the glass separately, and then two or three converged to form a small rivulet that started down the glass. Straight down they would plunge and suddenly veer obliquely away from their former course, only to change course again and plunge ever downward until they finally joined the water that was draining off the sill. Beyond the window the pines were indistinct shadows in the low mist that had come with the rain, and beyond the pines there was only empty space where I knew the lake was hidden in the gloom.

It was far from an ideal day, but there was no wind, and that was the important factor. Anyone who regularly fishes the lakes of the British Columbia interior comes prepared for the rain, and it was no obstacle. But there is little even the best fisherman can do against the wind when it becomes strong and violent.

The coffee pot on the wood stove perked sluggishly, then faster, and its fresh aroma joined the bacon scent. Altogether the cabin seemed a warm and cozy place that would be difficult to leave on such a day. But after breakfast was done and things were in order, I struggled into rain gear, took the rods from the rack on the wall and stepped outside. The sky and the forest still dripped in a fine, steady mist that was almost rain. The chill of the day was in sharp contrast to the warmth of the cabin, and I shivered involuntarily as I tried to adjust to the sudden difference in temperatures.

An overnight accumulation of rainwater shifted back and forth beneath the floorboards of the boat where I had left it at the dock the night before. Quick work with a bailing can eliminated most of it, and the outboard started quickly on the second pull. I slipped off the two lines that had held the boat fast to the dock and backed out into the bay. Ahead of me the wall of mist hid the expanse of the long lake.

It was perhaps a mile or a little more to the rocky shoal where I had found fish the day before. I opened the motor to full throttle and marveled as the mist absorbed its sound. The water seemed indistinct in the dull light, and only the waves peeling back from the bow, rolling out of sight in a great V behind me, were tangible evidence that I was traveling on water instead of air.

The shoal was hard to find in the dark morning light, and there was no visible evidence of it on the surface. I slowed the motor and searched in zigzag patterns until I saw the gravel looming up within a couple of feet of the surface. Moving slowly, I followed the gravel until I saw it slope sharply away into the depths, and there I cut the motor and dropped the anchor so I could cast from the shallows out over the drop-off. On a dark day such as this, I surmised, there was a chance that bigger fish would be moving. The rain was an irritant, but it was tolerable, and I looked forward with anticipation to the day.

The morning passed with mostly small fish taken and released and one heavy strike from an unseen fish that quickly disengaged itself from the fly. I ate a soggy lunch in the boat, lit my pipe with difficulty and resumed casting in the unabated rain. The rain came in surges, now falling heavily, now subsiding into mist but never ceasing altogether. The day remained dark, without color, without even blacks and whites, with only dull, contrasting shades of gray.

I cast the little shrimp fly out into the deep water, let it sink and then pulled it back with slow, even strips. Twice it was taken by fish, bright husky trout of about 14 inches each, which I played quickly to the boat and released after twisting the hook free from their jaws. After that, half a dozen casts produced nothing, so I pulled the anchor and moved farther down the shoal.

There I resumed casting, watching the dark line carry the little fly out into the mist, where it dropped in a little ring of water that was quickly lost in the rings made by the rain. I counted to myself while the fly sank, then began the familiar motion of the retrieve, and in this manner I searched the water in a semicircle around the anchored boat.

The afternoon was even less productive than the morning, and I found nothing but small fish as I worked my way along the shoal. The approach of evening was signaled only by a lessening of light, a darker gray, a deeper mist. Still I cast into the gloom, fishing mechanically now, my thoughts looking forward to the warmth of the stove in the cabin and the evening meal.

Suddenly the fly was stopped dead by an unyielding force, and before I could react the line was being taken away. It burned through the moisture on my finger as the fish ran until it was pulling line directly from the reel. I held on, with the breathless, helpless feeling that one always has when he realizes he has hooked a fish that is out of control. The backing splice was gone and the yellow coils of backing line were quickly following while the reel's scream reached a pitch I had never heard before.

Somewhere out in the gathering darkness and the rain I heard a great crash as the fish leaped and fell back at the end of its long run, and then I began the task of getting back the line it had taken. It came easily at first as the fish followed, but then it turned suddenly away, and the reel screamed as the fish ran farther into the backing. The next run ended with a second distant jump followed quickly by a third. Finally the fish settled down to slug it out, and I could feel it shaking its head viciously over the long line.

The backing line came back slowly to the reel until finally the splice showed above the surface. Suddenly a relaxation of pressure told me the fish was running toward me, and I reeled frantically until the run ended with a fourth leap not twenty feet away. I watched, enthralled, as the great trout tumbled end over end, high out of the water, its silver sides flashing through the rain.

Having shown itself, the fish was off on another run, taking with it most of the line I had regained, and I heard it jump again and thrash the surface far out. It resisted every turn of the reel, fought every movement of the rod and twice broke the surface with its broad tail. I worked it toward the boat slowly, and it swam in circles around the craft, refusing to be turned, forcing me to pivot and follow its movements. Another sudden run, another jump weaker than before; and for a moment its strength was gone, and I turned it and led it back. It recovered with the strength of desperation and turned suddenly and bore down toward the bottom, and I had to let it go.

Slowly, fighting its weight and ebbing strength, I forced it back toward the surface. It wallowed there and I swung it toward the boat. Again it swam away and down but with less strength, and this time I turned it against its will. Reluctantly, almost completely spent, it answered the pull of the line, came alongside the boat, thrashed once and tried to plunge away, then turned slowly on its broad side. I led it over the net and scooped it up in the heavy mesh, and it was too far spent to struggle any more.

I laid the fish down on the wet floorboards and looked at it. There was strength and beauty written in its shape; it was clean and bright and perfect silver, with only the first pale blush of rose along its flank. Its gills opened and closed in shuddering movements, and its great body quivered from exertion, and in its eyes was the look of wild, mortal fear.

I could not know that it was the Trout that had found its way up from the gravel of the little tributary; the same Trout that had sheltered and fed behind a small rock in the tributary's flow, then made its way through the August nights to the rich lake where it had lived so long. I knew nothing of its history, of the dangers it had endured, the hazards it had overcome.

I could not be aware of how its fellows had been reduced, one by one, until only a very few were left, or that this perhaps was the patriarch of them all. Its life was alien to me and would forever be. I could imagine, perhaps, what it had meant for this fish to live so long and grow so large, but I could not know.

Now its life was mine, if I chose to take it. A fish club was handy; in a single, swift blow I could erase all those long summers of life, all the wild freedom it had known. I could end the cycle that had begun in the dark gravel and which, if uninterrupted, would someday take the fish back to the same small place to begin the cycle once again. It was a trophy by any man's measure, a fish to remember, and one to be envied by my friends.

I reached for the club, but something stilled my hand. I still cannot fully fathom what it was. Perhaps it was the realization that it would be a highly selfish thing to terminate the cycle before it was complete. Perhaps it was the knowledge that within it this fish bore the seeds of strong progeny that would grow old and wild in their own time. Or, perhaps it was reluctance to take the life of a thing so beautiful and free.

For a long, awful moment, I was undecided. And then I knew what must be done.

Awkwardly, I retrieved the big fish from the net and twisted the fly out of the gristle of its jaw. I swung it over the side and placed it in the water, holding it steady with one hand, easing it back and forth with the other. The fish seemed to understand my purpose, and it waited patiently in my grasp as the movement of its gills slowly became regular once again. I felt the strength return to it with a sudden throb like an electric current running through its veins. I took my hands away and the fish was free. With a single stroke of its powerful tail it started forward and down, swimming slowly out of sight in the dark, rain-dotted water, and I was left alone with only the memory of our struggle.

I pulled the anchor, started the motor and turned the boat

toward the cabin. Far away through the darkness and the rain I could see the gleam of a lantern in the cabin window. Probably they would not believe me when I told them of the epic struggle or the size of the fish; I had let the evidence go free, and now the only evidence was in my memory. But I was happy; the memory was enough.

# The Hooker Hooked

ED ZERN

25

I caught my first trout at the age of five, from a mountain brook that flowed into the Cheat River in West Virginia not far from our summer cottage, using a piece of white wrapping string tied to a stick and a small safety pin on which I had impaled a cricket. It was a splendid brook trout, at least five inches long and beautifully formed and colored, and it fought fiercely, or would have if it hadn't been derricked onto the pine-needled bank the instant it bit the cricket; but on the way home I stopped to watch a man shoot a rattlesnake that had crawled under the porch of his cabin, and I lost the fish in my excitement.

That ended my trout fishing for a long time, as my family moved to a suburb of Pittsburgh, and the creeks that ran near my home flowed yellow and malodorous with coal-mine drainage. Summers I went to camps and caught smallmouth bass in Ontario, a brace of rather puny muskellunge in Conneaut Lake and one no larger in Lake Chautauqua, and various pickerel, perch, bullheads, walleyes, rock bass and sunnies in assorted waters. But no trout. I went to college surrounded by some of the best limestone creeks in Pennsylvania, when a limit of browns over two pounds with a five-pounder among them was no unusual feat, but it was in the midst of a depression—*the* depression— and a fishable split-cane fly-rod complete with reel and fly line cost upwards of ten dollars, which was more than I allowed myself for spending money for a month. (The three Leonard rods and Meek reels my father had left had been burned along with our house and most of its contents a few years previously.)

After college I shipped as a seaman on freighters for a year, then lucked my way into a writing job in a Philadelphia advertising agency. They paid me fifteen incredible dollars a week for a mere forty-four hours (the shipping line had paid me the going rate of $26.50 a month for a fifty-six-hour work-week, plus, of course, a bunk and food of sorts) and I saved enough during the first year to buy an extremely used Ford coupe for thirty-five dollars. One June day I was in the office of a senior vice-president of the company, and while waiting for him to finish a telephone call I studied a photograph on his wall, of him in a canoe netting a big squaretail.

"Like fishing?" he asked, when he had hung up.

"I do indeed," I said, "but it's a long time since I've done any."

"Ever fish for trout?" he asked.

"Only deep-water lakers," I said, "and it was too much like laying the Atlantic cable." I didn't feel I should count that five-incher.

"Got a car?" he asked, and when I said I did he changed the subject to business. The next Friday morning he called me up to his office and handed me an aluminum rod case in which was a three-piece eight-foot four-ounce Thomas rod, a reel with a silk double-tapered fly line on it, an envelope of leaders, a cardboard box with a dozen wet and dry flies in it and a pair of hip boots two sizes too large for me.

"Duck out at noon," he said, "and drive up 611 to East Stroudsburg. Take 209 there until you see a big frame hotel on the left, right beside the road, with a sign that says 'Charley's Hotel Rapids.' Go in and tell Charley I said for him to see that you catch some trout. Good luck."

I couldn't leave at noon because I had a lot of work to do, and in those days you didn't take chances with a job that paid that well. At five o'clock I rushed out, packed my sea-going dungarees and sweatshirt, which was the closest I could come to a sporting ensemble, and drove as fast as I could up 611. I found the hotel, a barnlike white-painted frame building so close to the D.L.&W. railroad tracks that the building shuddered and shook when trains roared by, and went in and introduced myself to Charley Rethoret, a stumpy, volatile, fierce-looking Alsatian with a ragged mustache. When I gave him the message from Wes Gilman he assigned me to a room upstairs and told me to change clothes and come back down. It was nearly dark, but I got into my dungarees and boots and went back down. Charley seemed startled at my outfit and asked if I had ever fished for trout. I said no, and he thought for a minute, then said okay, he thought he could help me catch a trout.

On the porch outside the bar I set the rod up while Charley pawed through the flies Wes had lent me and picked out a fairly large White Miller, probably a #6. I had tied a heavy leader to the line because that was the only kind Wes had lent me, but Charley said no, that's not the right leader, and went back of the bar into a cigar box and dug up a much lighter one, probably 3X or 4X. When he had tied the fly to it he handed me the outfit and a flashlight—it was now quite dark—and led me across the tracks to the top of a high bank beside the creek.

"Take that path down to the water," Charley said, "and right at the bottom there's a boulder with an iron spike in it. It's all that's left of an old footbridge. Cast your fly straight out from there about two rod lengths, no more, and let it swing in the current until it's straight downstream. Don't use the light unless you have to. Don't use more than ten feet of line or you'll get hung up behind you. Keep doing that until something happens."

"What if nothing happens?" I said.

Charley shrugged. "Then come back and have a drink and dinner," he said, and walked back across the tracks to the hotel, where several other cars had pulled up since I had arrived.

I slid cautiously down the steep path to the water, not using the light at all. By the time I had felt my way to the creek my pupils had dilated, and I could dimly see a boulder at the water's edge, with an iron spike stuck in it.

I peeled about six feet of line off the reel and flipped the fly awkwardly into the water. When it had swung downstream I peeled off a few more feet and flipped it out again. The third time I flipped the fly onto the dark, rushing water I saw something swirl violently in the current, making a wave almost a foot high, and at the same instant there came a yank on the line that nearly tore the rod from my hand, and no doubt would have if the leader hadn't popped like a rotten thread.

I was too dumbfounded to do anything but sit down on the boulder and light a cigarette with trembling fingers. When the cigarette was finished I walked back up the bank to the hotel, changed clothes and sat down to one of those "Analomink Charley" meals that drew nonfishermen from a hundred miles around and helped to make up for the abominable beds and the noise and cinders of the railroad. By the time Charley came by to ask how I had done, the whole episode seemed somehow unreal, but when I told him what had happened he didn't seem at all surprised. "Better luck next time," he said cheerfully and hurried off to greet Gene Connett or George LaBranche or Jack Knight or Preston Jennings or Jim Leisenring or some other now-legendary figure of the trout-fishing world, none of whom I had then ever heard of but some of whom it would be my great privilege to know and to fish with in coming seasons on the Brodheads.

For although I didn't know it at the time, I had been hooked as surely and solidly as that big brown trout; and although he probably rubbed the hook out of his jaw that same night, I've never recovered from the one he stuck into me.

It wasn't until I had fished that splendid little river for several seasons and had come to know Charley Rethoret well that I realized why he had made me use a light leader that night. He believed that a few really big trout give a stream character and give fishermen something to talk about, and he saw no reason to risk having a novice angler horse one of his biggest trout out of

the home pool. (When I wanted to try for Leviathan another night, Charley asked me not to, giving some totally implausible reason, and I never did.)

Charley's gone now, and the hotel's gone, and the skinny kid in dungarees with the borrowed tackle has been transformed into something grosser and grayer and grouchier, even if better equipped. But the river's still there, having survived even the Army Corps of Engineers after one big flood, and it may be that the big trout's great-great-great-great-great-great-great-grandson is finning himself in the current behind that same midstream boulder. I hope so.

# *Reverie with an Old Fishing Vest*

ANGUS CAMERON



Every angler knows that the events and circumstances of life, of every life, include a host of things more momentous, more significant and important to him, than anything that ever happened to him on a stream or lake or river. A first meeting with one's beloved, a look through a hospital pane at one's newborn child, some triumph of creation or inventiveness, some time-tested achievement—a host of important moments surely can crowd out and label as trivial (or at least of lesser meaning) what may have happened to him a long-gone day when a bit of intensely private angling history was made, yet it is left there. I suppose one could say that the delights of the senses may be neutral, that emotional sensibility is without discrimination, a delicious leveler as willing to recall a trivial delight to the same level of vivid memory as a truly momentous event of overweening life significance.

This neutrality of sensual recall permits the grateful angler to remember his high moments of angling as full peers with those others of greater import to the course of his life. And all of us have a marvelous succession of them, too. Indeed what fisherman cannot mount a glittering, full-dressed parade of them with his eyes closed and ear pressed against his "deaf pillow"? Leaping trout are the sheep of the angler's sleep-inducing dreams.

As an angler of lowly beginnings and modest means—I owned a second-magnitude Pflueger Summit and yearned for a Supreme—I had long dreamed of becoming a fly fisherman. However, as I had only slowly evolved from bamboo pole and bait to a True Temper casting rod, it could have been predicted that it would take a while for me to get nerve enough even to aspire to a fly rod. At last I did hesitantly buy a #14 South Bend fly rod, and I remember my amazement when I took my first bass with it out of a flat stretch on old Flat Rock that I had passed up for years as too shallow for bass.

As mentioned before I did "graduate" to trout, but I always felt a bit of an upstart in the lofty company of my betters, even after I had become a fairly decent trout angler. But even then there was a heaven of a further magnitude peopled by rare beings that I may have worshiped from afar but, knuckling my forehead in obeisance, dared not aspire to join. I refer, of course, to salmon fishermen. The pictures I saw of them always showed them as sartorially correct and, I suspected, exceedingly well-off gentlemen whose glories were often captioned something like this: "The author with three salmon over fifteen pounds each taken successively on his (l. to r.) Leonard, Payne, and Orvis rods, also pictured here . . . the reels are Hardys, of course." How could a man who began on mud pouts and sunnies expect to rise to such company? But the lowly do aspire, and finally emboldened by my trout fishing and by age, perhaps, I finally got up enough nerve to plan a salmon trip. Not to a camp where real angling aristocrats consort but to a more democratic scene—

the Matane; here one paid a rod fee and could hide his novice antics somewhere along a 22-mile stretch of pools.

I had intended to go alone but at the last minute a classics scholar friend of mine who had never fished in his life decided to step in where angels feared to wade and to *begin* his angling career on salmon! Whenever I think of his heroic initiation I think of him as a man fully fit to associate daily as he does with Achilles or Hector. Not that he caught a salmon; he didn't, but he fearlessly exposed himself to the noble fish, and he did learn to cast and took several trout.

However, I did take a salmon, and when I think of what had happened before that greatest moment of all I feel the hackles crawl on the back of my neck and a slight, hot sensation on the edges of each shoulder blade.

Although the vividness of my memory seems to say that I was born for that moment the fact is that I prepared for it—improperly for the most part. For instance, I tied up a storm of salmon flies, mostly Cameron variants on the classic British patterns—with feathers poorly married and much too fully dressed. I tied these flies portentously, fully aware as the components were tied into place that "this one might be it!" Sometime, probably on a June Sunday morning, on my glassed-in sun porch I tied the fatal fly.

I had said to my daughter during one of those fly-tying sessions, "One of these flies will hook my first salmon." I probably said it fatefully, without irony and surely without humor. I must have cut a pretty ridiculous figure plonking down such a sententious prophecy. Although I don't remember how my daughter reacted to this parental fatuousness, I do know that it must have been respectful, for I was in such a state of anticipation that levity would not have been tolerated. She did say something, however, that I do remember. She said, "Why don't you make a fly with feathers colored like the Cameron tartan?" It was just the sort of suggestion to bring out the sentimental worst in me, although the bastard fly itself did not seem to suffer. I dubbed it Cathie's Erracht-Cameron fly and placed it and a copy (not so good a job) in my fly box.

One day last fall after the season was over I decided to look again on that most notable fly. I went confidently to my tackle kit, found the box I was sure that housed the relic, but could not find the fly. I then began a frantic search, upsetting the house-

hold in the process. At last, frustrated, I turned to my wife, who, with that fantastic genius of a well-ordered mind, said, "It's in your fly vest."

"No, no," I said with ill patience, "I have already looked there."

"The old fly vest," she said, with full patience of wifely control.

Sheepishly I remembered that I had let a friend wear that vest on the Miramichi the previous September and probably had let him fish out of that very box. (It was foolish of me for it contained my old flies.) Sure enough, the box was there and so was the fly, but of course it took me awhile to find the old vest.

I found it hanging on the back of the rough wooden door to our attic, and I realized it had not been used by me for a dozen years. It was on a wire hanger and still looked rather spruce and undisheveled. I looked at it with affection and thought. Occasionally I stuff it in a duffel or Duluth bag to serve some novice friend making his first fishing junket, but I never wear it any more. It's not worn out, just retired. Indeed, save for a fraying of the cuffs, the fine-weave cotton material from which it is made looks in much better shape than that of many a newer poplin-like garment I own.

In an inside, left-hand pocket I found a flat aluminum leader box still equipped with two wetting pads, now hard-dried and wrinkled with disuse. A musty smell of bygone mildew reminded me of how many times I had washed out these same pads in the days when leaders were made of gut and had to be wetted before use.

I am not military-minded these days, but I thought of the old vest as a kind of uniform, a garment that would perhaps not pass muster in an inspection now but was nonetheless the veteran of a hundred actions of great moment to its owner. I thought that maybe there ought to be several gay spectrums of service bars above its left breast pocket (pockets!). Yes, that would be most appropriate.



The vest triggered memories of some fine moments we (the vest and I) had not shared, of course, like the day my cousin Kenny and I caught the fabulous string of sun fish in old Herrigan. I can remember how it felt to hoist that dripping stringer of twenty-six man's hand-sized red-eared sunfish; just as I can remember how it felt to walk barefoot in cool, rain-pattered dust in a country lane. But can I make someone else feel it? All I can say is that I was "knee deep in June," the day was all sun and fleecy clouds, and the red-orange, blue-green, five-by-five plumpness of those gorgeous sunnies raised that boy's spirits to heights of ecstasy. I can see them now turning slowly as the twist came out of the stringer, displaying now gold-bronze gleam of sides, now black-green backs and then the brilliant orange, pristine roundness of their "throats." That memory has lasted sweetly for a lifetime, but it was superseded by another just a summer later. And how long between summers in those bygone Hoosier days.

A hot August morning had challenged my father and me from the first. The spade turned up few worms until it struck the manured surface beneath the eaves in the shade of an old chicken house where enough moisture remained to hold the succulent worms near the surface. Two Prince Albert tobacco cans were full at last! My Dad carried his in his right hip pocket. I carried mine the same way and with some pride for I had discovered for the first time that I had hip pockets.

We fished down Herrigan with scant success. We crossed the ironweed-bordered field near the mouth and came out onto the larger creek, Flat Rock. "We'll hit her at the Gas Pipe," my father said. The magic words: *the Gas Pipe!* I knew from tales my father and my uncles told that this place was fabled for its good fishing—a far, far Oregon to a farm-bound boy who had never ventured nearly this far alone.

Shortly after we made our way across a cornfield, over a fence and through a "hedge apple" row, the great, white, frothy cumulus clouds that had been building up all afternoon turned dark, then black. They opened with a spatter of great drops that soon mounted to a wild torrent. The glistening rain made a slanting white sheet that was whipped wildly across Flat Rock by a rising wind. Dad and I had dropped our rods against some low saplings and taken a dubious refuge beneath the trees in the hedge row. He threw an arm across my wet shoulders, and I remember a gush of affection and relief, then a poignant coziness made up of the roughness and warmth of my father's tweed jacket against my cheek. I recall with this an odor, which comes back to me now, as a lovely mix of my Dad's familiar smell, a healthy whiff of wet wool and the peppery fragrance of pipe tobacco.

As I huddled against my father the storm raged. The high wind, the zigzag of lightning close by and the near simultaneous crashes of thunder brought that storm nearer than any I had ever experienced before. Suddenly the wind that had swayed the tops of the walnut trees and pressed over the tall corn in a field behind slackened and then quit. The wind's running dog, the thunder, growling meanly, rumbling sullenly as it rolled away, seemingly frustrated that these two sodden humans had somehow remained immune to the fury of its display.

Soon all was over: only the slow drip of water off the leaves broke the sudden silence. "Well, son," my dad said, "we'll now see whether the storm has spoiled the fishing or improved it." Regaining our gear—Dad's, a metal rod with a *real* reel on it, mine, a long bamboo pole—we crossed the limestone-bottomed creek at a wide shallow and made our way down to a favorite hole commanded by the overhanging roots of a dead sycamore. The fishing was sensational. Five rock bass, big wide, solid ones eight inches long, came quickly to the stringer. And then, wonder of wonders, my dad caught a bass! It was a fourteen-inch largemouth, not only the first black bass I had ever seen but also the largest fish of any kind. It seemed a miracle to me. After admiring it before and after it was on the stringer and being awed with its huge mouth and underslung and predatory lower jaw, I returned to my own fishing.

Not a minute later, it happened. My red-and-green bobber went under, came up slowly, then went down and away, clear out of sight. Eyes popping, I stared in fascination. The eddy-slacked line was soon used up; then I felt the surge of power from this evident monster. Galvanized at last, I heaved upward on my pole with two hands, and I was dismayed that at first the power I had applied was brought stock-still. Then the fish gave against such leverage and sailed out, up and over into the ironweeds behind. I can still feel the sensation of scrabbling on hands and knees in the high weeds to recover this fabulous twelve-inch fish. My father's words echo back across the years, "Well, son, you can always remember that you were eleven years old when you caught your first bass."

Those two moments took place years before I got the old fishing vest. My wife bought it for me for Christmas, 1938, from Jim Deren when he had the old place in the loft on 45th Street.

(My wife reminds me that she bought me a pair of waders that same Christmas and it took her from the night before Christmas until two days after April Fool's Day to get a bill out of Jim for the two items.)

I bought a bamboo fly rod the following spring and, armed with Ray Bergman's *Trout* as my only mentor, took off for the Catskills in search of the famous fish. We made a lot of trips up old Route 17, and I fished the Neversink and the Rondout a full spring of weekends without catching a single trout. The old snapshots of me in my Hodgmans and many-pocketed vest, waist-deep in the Neversink around Claryville, make me appear a quite legitimate trout angler. I was, but I was troutless.

I caught my first trout the next spring, a thirteen-inch rainbow in a little stream a few miles from Burlington, Vermont, with a streamer fly. I remember it very well but somehow it doesn't really stand out with me. Could it be that this important happening was dimmed for me by the fact that shortly after the capture of my first trout my wife caught a wind-blown streamer in her scalp? The fact that she cut the leader and fished another half hour before deciding that maybe we'd better go in and let a doctor remove it does have some overshadowing potentials, I suppose.

But the old vest was on me when I hooked the big rainbow on the Sehoharie. Its pocket carried the box that housed the first fly I ever tied, and it witnessed the miracle that same fly performed above the Croton bridge at Brewster by taking an eleven-inch brown the very first time it was cast!! I wore the old garment that cold May morning on Grand Lake Stream when I first felt the wild power of a landlocked salmon fast to a Supervisor. It went to Alaska with me and shared those pink-blue visions called grayling. It went with me to the Kepimits in central Labrador's virgin waters and witnessed the taking of three squaretails over four pounds in a single day's fishing.

As I retrieved the fly box and put the old vest back on the back of the attic door I regretted that I had not worn it on that first trip to the Matane. "I should have worn it," I thought rather boobishly to myself. I put the fly box back in my kit bag, but held out Cathie's Erracht-Cameron fly. I decided I would have my wife frame it (*she* has a miter box and can do things like that); it would remind me of that first fishing trip for salmon. Of course, I had to admit that that fly was a rather embarrasing reminder.

For you must understand that at the time I knew absolutely nothing about salmon fishing. True, I had a copy of Lee Wulff's *Atlantic Salmon* with me, and I had enviously and hopelessly perused a good deal of British salmon-fishing literature over the years, but my friend Arthur knew more about such similarly esoteric subjects as the optimates membership in the Roman Senate just prior to Caesar's crossing of the Rubicon than I knew about taking the lordly salmon. (He was re-reading *Caesar's Gallic Wars* as a quick boneup for the coming fall semester.)

I will never forget that first morning on the Matane. We took off from our cabin camp (they were *not* motels on the Matane in those days) and drove, unerringly, as I later learned, to a section of the river whose succession of beautiful-*looking* pools did not include a single holding or resting pool. I had noticed that some of the pools were named and marked by the Matane Salmon Association, but I had not realized that there were few holding pools that were not marked by the M.S.A. As a result we fished for three days (the marked pools always seemed to have an angler already in them) in beautiful pools that had never rested, let alone held, a salmon in the memory of man. But never mind—I cast these barren pools as happily as may be, laid down and fished out my 160-odd casts an hour a good seven hours a day and fancied, by paying heed to Lee's advices, that I was learning to fish a wet fly. My wife says I am a gloomy philosopher of men's affairs but an optimist when it comes to fishing. It is true; no amount of failure ever tarnishes the bright expectancy I feel as each cast goes out and fishes down and across. Hope springs not only eternal in a steady glow from this breast but also from second to second and minute to minute in a series of tiny, bright, cheerful quanta of expectancies.



Knowing little or nothing about salmon fishing, I willingly accepted my failure to raise a single fish as the penalty of ignorance and lack of skill. My classicist friend, Arthur, wearing, by the way, my old fishing vest, would cast an hour or so, and then if not even a trout rewarded him would retire to the shady side of a shoreline tree and read in one of the Loeb Classics he had with him.

With me in the river and my companion reading Latin

across the stream from me, I was sometimes reminded of a steel engraving headpiece in a favorite edition of *The Compleat Angler* that bucolically recorded just such a scene. Although I had not raised a single fish, "I was not hurtin'," as they say. I was, in truth, having the time of my life. I had seen no fish in the river (and no wonder), but I had seen and been intimidated by a twenty-one-pound fish on display on the floor of a car trunk in the parking lot of a nearby tavern. Although I could not understand the lucky angler's French, Arthur could, and it was here that we began to get the notion that all the pools that glittered did not necessarily hold gold or, in this case, the silver of resting salmon. Because I did not care to fish the well-marked and always well-attended resting pools near the road, I needed the advice of some local about other pools, perhaps a bit more remote, if of lesser reputation.

Our landlord sent us down the road *un peu* to a local angler whose English was far better than my French and who not only told us about, but also took us to, two pools. Not the best, he said, but good enough to be worth fishing, and they had the virtue of being far enough away from the road that I never saw another angler that year or succeeding ones while fishing these pools. Our new friend showed us the lies, spoke briefly about how to fish each pool and then left us to our own devices. As I looked across the wide, smooth and deepish run, I saw where a mile-long deadwater above fell off in a faster but still smooth glide toward an angling riffle. The riffle separated the tail of this spacious upper pool from the narrow, faster and deeper run of the lower that I could make out curving away downstream.

I waded out into the tail of the upper pool, just below the riffle, crossed an eddied bay to the gravelly shore of the lower pool, and stepping out a yard or so into the current laid Cathie's Erracht-Cameron across and downstream. The fly, although not hitched, nevertheless cut a tiny V as it swung its arc below me. Before I could think to slow its pace by mending lines, the fly had drifted around and was dangling straight downstream. For some reason, perhaps in the drawn-out reverie of a sightless stare at the bewitching waters, I made no move to lift the fly out and cast again.

It was at this moment that something seized the fly with a frantic pull of such awesome strength that a surge of what I later identified as pure, unalloyed terror coursed down my spine. My reaction, dread *over*reaction, was to pull back just as frantically. For a moment, a split second, only the rod moved—mediator between me and the fish—in a vicious downward arc, and then with what I felt was a rasping, scratchy feeling the fly came away. As it did a great lump of water rose where the fly had been and broke in a loud slurp, making a big hole. A great silvery fish rolled slowly out of this hole and turned lazily over on its side, revealing as it did so its noble depth and length. Its motion was slow-motion save for a wicked, sweeping splash of its broad tail as it disappeared. Then the disturbance was washed clean by the big current, eddied away in little swirls until nothing was left of the astonishing drama. Only the thump of my heart pounding in my chest remained.

I spoke aloud, in measured tones, "That—must—have—been—a—salmon." Then, as the reality hit me, "My God a'mighty, it *was* a salmon!"

As I think about it now and, as I feel about it again, I know that, in a way, everything that has happened since has been measured against that first strike. An hour afterward in the big glide above the riffle I hooked and landed my first salmon. It was a grilse, a big one, that jumped thirteen times by my count. Arthur watched me from the far shore—even rose from his reading—to watch the twenty-minute battle.

As we walked back to the car he said, "You know, just as you yelled when this fish took I was reading the section where Pompey pulled off his general's vestments and took flight after the rout at Pharsalus."

Do you think for a moment his reference to that earth-shaking event put that first strike back into proper proportion as trivial? I looked at my four-pound, two-ounce grilse with pleasure, but I could not, of course, forget that great fish of an hour before. I thought to myself, "Caesar won the battle *and* the war at Pharsalus; I won the battle but lost the war on the Matane."

I told you that emotional recall is a great leveler, that it can raise a trivial delight to the same level of significance as many a more important event. More important event? Name one more important than one's first strike from an Atlantic salmon.

# The Wee Stick

JACK SAMSON



It hadn't rained for three months in Scotland. Arthur Oglesby, the European editor for *Field & Stream,* met A. J. McClane and me at the airport in Edinburgh as we can came in from London after a nine-hour flight from New York.

We had come to Scotland in the last part of September for the salmon fishing and a few days of shooting driven pheasants and red-legged partridge. We had carried our cased, light rods aboard the plane—much to the consternation of the stewardesses, who probably thought they were cue sticks for an international billiard match or sword canes with which to hijack the jet to Dublin.

Arthur was not in the best of spirits when we disembarked at Edinburgh. He is a fine trout and salmon fisherman, and the author of a number of books on the subject. He is also a constant contributor to the *Fishing Times* and *Shooting Times* of London. It was not the early hour that disturbed him, but the low water. No true fisherman is happy when the chances of catching fish are poor.

"Awfully sorry," Arthur said, in what must have been the understatement of the century. "The damned rivers are all low, and if a salmon took a fly, it would be because it had gone daft."

I looked at McClane and he at me. Both of us being of Scotch ancestry, there was not much else to say.

"Do you suppose," said McClane, "there would be a good inn that had fine kippers on the way north?"

"Now, there," answered Oglesby, "is the first intelligent question we have come to. I think I can guarantee that."

With due ceremony we stashed the rod cases and gear in the car and headed north.

The Tweed was indeed a disaster. We stayed in a fine hotel—where the kippers were as good as reputed—and both McClane and I spent a fruitless hour and a half trying to interest some tired salmon which had been lying in the same pool for months. None showed the slightest inclination to rise to a fly, although they periodically jumped as salmon on a spawning run will do. The Tweed is a magnificent river; but it is one which will break the heart of a fly fisherman when it is too low, and the salmon are not in a taking mood.

We ended up driving back to Edham House and enjoyed a fine hour or so talking to other disgruntled fishermen who had been there for weeks and had not had a strike. The English and the Scots seemed to have a lot more perseverance than North American trout and salmon fishermen. It may be because when the fish are not striking these men have no other place to go on their tight little island, while North American anglers can take off for provinces or rivers reputed to be better. At any rate, we all agreed there was no question about the reason for the lack of activity. The streams were extremely low and the fish had been staying in the holding pools for a long time. Even when they jumped one could see that they were getting dark red—almost black—and were late spawners.

The following morning we drove farther north and stopped at noon on the Tay to see what it was like. The river was one of the most beautiful I have ever seen, but it, too, was very low, and the fishermen we met at the local inn at lunch had the same report that the men had on the Tweed—low water and no action.

The only option left was to drive as far north as we could and hope to catch the run on the Spey, on the northeast coast. The salmon there might still be coming in from the North Sea and might be less affected by the low water and lack of rainfall.

We arrived late that night at Seafield Estates, a fine shooting and fishing preserve at Cullen, a beautiful, small town on the sea coast. No one had time to get acquainted at that ungodly hour of the night, but the host, Eric Yates, had the foresight to leave the bar open with instructions that we be revived with some of the excellent Scotch whisky from the many distilleries dotting the landscape of northern Scotland. It probably saved our lives after the seven-hour drive across the moors.

The following morning found us on the Spey, one of the most magnificent rivers I have ever seen. The late-September weather had turned the aspen and birch leaves to gold and red and the water, low as it was, was filled with salmon fresh from the North Sea and on their way up the great stream. They had been coming into the Spey since spring—a continuing surge of life.

At about ten A.M. we arrived at the stretch of the Spey which our host had said was the best of the approximately twenty-seven miles of the river owned by the estate. Our ghillie was a man named Georgie Williams, a dour-looking Scot whose looks belied his nature. Dressed in the traditional knickers and stalking cap, he looked at my tiny 3⅜-ounce, seven-foot, split-bamboo fly rod and shook his head.

"You're not goin' to do much on this river, lad," he said, "with that wee stick."

McClane had a seven-foot glass rod which weighed only an ounce or so more than mine. Because we had been converting big-rod men for years from the Bahamas to Quebec, I said nothing. I did note, however, that Arthur had unleashed his twelve-foot English "telephone pole" and had waded into the rapids. I found out in the first few moments, however, that Arthur could do a roll cast with the big rod that was called the "Spey cast" and literally shot the line across the big river.

I am sure the big rod is a great advantage—especially in the spring when the water is high. But I cannot help it; I am a light-tackle devotee. I had run into the same situation in Iceland the previous August. The English had all been fishing with the big rods and keeping all the salmon they caught. Salmon was then selling for about two dollars a pound on the market in Reykjavik. I had been fishing for a week with Lee Wulff and his wife Joan and releasing every salmon I caught. The Icelandic guides thought I was insane. But the day I left I was told by one of our hosts, a member of the Icelandic Salmon Club: "The English taught us how to *catch* the salmon years ago. You Americans have taught us the sport of salmon fishing." That was reward enough.

It was not more than half an hour before Arthur had a strike and was hooked up. We all waded ashore to watch the battle. The fish was a good one, and Georgie stood behind Arthur and said very little, recognizing an expert at work when he saw one.

After about ten minutes the fish began to tire, and Arthur brought it into the shallows. It was a beautiful fish, about eight pounds, still silvery from the salt water and full of strength. Georgie tailed it and held it up for photographs before we released it to swim back into the current. Arthur went back upstream to try for another, and Georgie, with a pitying glance at McClane and me, retired to a wooden bench to smoke his pipe and watch us cast. I had tied on a nondescript black wet fly which had been tied by a first-class trout and salmon angler back home, Eric Peper. He never did tell me what it was called, nor did I ever ask. It looked a bit like a Green Butt, and he told me it had worked for him on the Miramichi.

I had a 30-foot shooting-head fly-line on the small reel with 75 feet of 20-pound monofilament tied to it with a nail knot. The backing was 100 yards of 18-pound-test braided Dacron. With it I was able to cast a pretty fair distance; a fact that did not escape the notice of Georgie, although he did not make any great effort of acknowledging it.

If he ignored my casting, he made a special effort to show disinterest at A. J.'s casts—which were reaching close to the far

bank. There are not many fly fishermen in the world that can equal the McClane when it comes to heaving a fly. Arthur knew this as did I, but we had not so informed Georgie. He did notice it, however, and missed a few puffs on the pipe when Al made a particularly beautiful cast—which was often.

The take on my cast to a bit of rough water was as gentle a take as I have felt in many a year of salmon fishing. The fish never broke water. If I had not fished for Atlantic salmon before, I might have thought I was hung up on a snag. But, knowing the ways of the fish, I set the hook gently and waited to see what would happen. As I expected, there was a slight movement to the middle of the stream as the fish felt the hook. I had no butt extension on the tiny rod and raised it high overhead and cupped the reel with my left hand for the expected run.

"Hey!" A. J. shouted from above me and began backing out of the river, reeling in his line to give me room. "Fish on!"

Arthur splashed ashore from below me as Georgie got up from the bench and strolled casually down to the shore behind me.

"Now, don't fight him too hard, lad," he cautioned. "That wee stick will never hold him if he takes it into his head to run downstream."

A. J. had moved down beside me and was unlimbering a camera to get some action shots. He winked as I glanced at him, and I felt better. The little rod had not let me down on the Miramichi, the George and the Icelandic rivers. I was fairly sure it wasn't going to fail me on the Spey—Georgie or no Georgie.

The salmon came out of the middle of the current suddenly when it finally realized it was in trouble. The reel whirred, and the handle scoured my palm as I cupped it. The little rod bent double as the fish headed downstream, and I moved to my left—trying to keep a footing on the slippery and rocky bottom of the Spey.

"He's going into the big pool below, lad," Georgie shouted, doing a semi-dance behind me. "Keep the tip as high as you can." (If the tip had been any higher I would have looked like Wilt Chamberlain.)

The fish made a spectacular jump—switching ends in midair—and came down with a resounding splash.

"Oh, look at him, look at him!" Georgie shouted. "What a beauty!"

I was too busy at the moment to appreciate the local dialect. The fish was fairly heavy. I couldn't tell how big it was, but it was a nice fish, and the river current wasn't helping me as much as it was the fish.

The salmon made several more jumps, but I really wasn't worried too much about losing it for lack of line, what with the backing on the small reel. My only real worry was that it might find a sharp rock or underwater snag.

I kept moving downstream and was followed by a retinue of ghillie, Arthur and A. J. taking pictures. I began to notice my right arm was tiring from the strain, but that was nothing new with a good fish on. One thing about the small rods—they are fun, but they don't give one any chance to rest.

"There's a bar down about thirty yards," Georgie cautioned. "If you can keep him in the big pool for a while until he tires, we can perhaps lead him onto the sand—as long as you can hold him with that bit of a rod," he hastened to add.

At this point Arthur laughed. "I have a feeling, Georgie," he said, "that wee stick, as you call it, is going to be enough."

Georgie grunted something in Scottish, which I was too busy to try and translate.

The fish fought long, and it fought well, as do all Atlantic salmon. When it finally tired and got close to the sand bar, I waded out to try to get it close to me. Suddenly I realized that Georgie was wading beside me—leather shoes, woolen stockings, knickers and all. I was wearing chest waders.

"Now, now, lad," Georgie said softly. "Lead him a bit toward me. Easy now, *easy!* Don't rush him . . . easy, easy . . ."

He had no tailer, just his hands. I began to watch him, rather than the fish. He was bending over from the waist and staring into the water, carefully watching the fish.

"Aye, aye," he advised, "Just a bit closer now. Ease that wee stick a bit to the left. Aye, that's it. Just a bit more now, lad. Fine, fine . . ."

And suddenly he reached down and had the salmon by the tail—a fine, beautiful, vibrant, silvery fish of about twelve pounds—wriggling as he held it aloft. I heard Arthur's jubilant shout from behind me and also heard the repeated clicks as A. J. took pictures of us both standing thigh-deep in the cold, calm, clear water.

And after that it was putting the beautiful fish back into the shallows—moving it back and forth until the gills worked well, until it swam strongly, and finally letting it go back into the mainstream to join its upward-bound brethren.

I reeled in the line and sloshed out onto the grassy bank.

"Georgie," I said, "what in the hell did you have to wade into that freezing river for? It's going to take you hours to dry out."

Georgie stamped his feet for a bit on the sod and grinned. "If this water could have hurt a member of the Williams family it would have killed my great-grandfather and his alike, all the way down to me. We've been ghillies on this river for a great many generations."



Arthur laughed and beckoned us to the wooden bench up on the bank.

"I have a little toast," he said, "seeing as this is your first salmon in Scotland."

He had put four tiny silver shot-sized glasses on the bench and was filling them with Scotch whisky, seventy proof and distilled not more than seventy miles from where we were standing. He handed Georgie four more plastic cups The ghillie, without any need of instruction, walked down to the edge of the river and filled all four with water from the Spey.

We all raised the glasses and I caught the twinkle in Georgie's eye.

"To your first Scottish salmon, laddie," he said. "May it never be your last."

I swallowed the whisky and followed it with a sip of Spey water.

The warmth spread in my stomach and I grinned at the tall Englishman and the wiry Scot, standing in his soaking shoes, socks and knickers.

"If it's my last, Georgie," I said. "It will be enough."

We all emptied the tiny silver glasses as the noontime sun glinted on the surface of the Spey and the incredibly clean September air blew in from the North Sea.

# Four Rivers in Iceland

LEE WULFF



When an old-time fly fisherman finds something akin to the once available but long since vanished wild fishing of a quarter of a century ago, he has cause for rejoicing. As late as the fifties any angler who was willing to pack in or fly in to the remote pools on the Newfoundland and Labrador rivers could find streams where he might have a stretch of river to himself, raise a dozen Atlantic salmon in a day, and find himself engaged, occasionally, in a contest with a fish of more than twenty pounds.

Since that time, not only have the crowds overrun the relatively inexpensive public fishing rivers, but the nets of commercial fishermen near the rivermouths or on the high seas have so overharvested the Atlantic salmon that even on the most exclusive private rivers like the Restigouche, salmon fishing has been reduced to very few and much smaller fish.

In Iceland the story has been just the opposite. Icelanders have always controlled their rivers and their salmon runs, with the "take" being regulated and the harvesting being done by permission (at a price) from the owner. Very limited netting has taken place in the tidal rivers, but there has been no netting in the sea, and no one has yet found the sea-feeding grounds of the Icelandic salmon schools. The many Icelanders who fish have, till now, found the angling within their means and the salmon plentiful. In the last few seasons, however, the angling world has discovered Iceland's salmon rivers, and angling fees are skyrocketing. Icelandic angling is still a good bargain, but the fees for nonresidents are due to continue to soar in the coming years.

This past summer, 1972, my wife, Joan Salvato, and I were able to fish on four of Iceland's many rivers, and here is our report.

## *The Laxa Adaldal*

This river is that rarity among salmon rivers, a stream with a controlled flow. Water from a lake drains through a hydro-power plant where the flow can be regulated. Warm springs seep in to mix with the cold flow from the snow-capped mountains and hold the temperature cooler in summer, warmer in winter, avoiding the extremes of hot and cold that most rivers must endure. The food supply is good. The fish run larger than in most of the icelandic rivers, and a fair share of thirty-pounders can be dependent upon in the annual run.

On the debit side, the river has few beaches to wade on and cast from, and the underwater growth is luxurious. The latter supports a great food source for the fingerling salmon, but during late July and August, when a salmon is hooked, he's almost certain to break off some clusters of weeds as he runs with the line, and an angler soon finds himself playing not only a fish but heavy sodden gobs of green stuff as well. A heavier leader helps with the problem, but only by repeatedly freeing the line of its green burden can the average salmon be brought to hand.

My guide was Heimir Sigurdsson, a gray-haired farm owner who owned one of the best pools on the river and had spent most of his many summers either guiding or fishing for salmon. He knew the river as well as a man could know it, and when he suggested that I cast just six feet below a certain rock and five feet this side of it, I knew the odds were ten to one there'd be a salmon lying under my fly.

Icelandic streams have few fly hatches and relatively little insect life in them. Traditionally the fishing is by wet fly in the conventional manner and with the standard patterns the British anglers brought when they first began Iceland's angling almost a century ago.

Being a nonconformist on flies I started out with a shrimp fly with gray mallard wings and *blaze orange* hackle legs. Heimir shook his head when I tied the fly on. He gulped a little when, on the fifth cast, a salmon rose to look it over—and swallowed hard when, a little later, the fish took the fly. In spite of his leaps and runs, which drew out considerable backing, and some weeds that weighted the line during his final moves, he came, tired, to the shallows.

Heimir, in short boots, stood ready on the shore with his long-handled net, but I held the fish to the waist-deep water where I stood, a dozen feet from shore, until I could tail him with my hand. I carried him ashore and put him in the net.

I wanted Heimir to recognize my independence of thought as to flies and methods and my competence as an angler. This done, I sat down with him, opened two fly boxes, and asked him to choose the best fly for the day and the pool. He picked a Jock Scott number eight, double, one of the few double-hooked flies in my vest. I tied it on and headed back into the stream.

Half an hour later a salmon, after three false rises, took the fly solidly and streaked for the open water of the great pool that stretched away downstream. He picked up pounds of weeds and dragged them around behind him. I was glad I'd followed Heimir's advice and used a fifteen-pound-test leader instead of my usual six or eight. I could scarcely feel the shock of the salmon's leaps on the line. The clinging weeds absorbed them—absorbed them so abruptly that I understood why many of the Laxa anglers go to twenty- and even thirty-pound leaders.

By getting below the fish, the current would slowly slide the greenery within reach, where, when I had a hand to spare, it could be torn apart and discarded. Three weedings and the line stayed clean. The weeds, as well as my playing, had tired the fish, and at the end of ten minutes I led him over Heimir's net. He weighed in later at thirteen pounds; just average for the Laxa. In the days that followed I learned that on some days the river flowed almost weed-free, while on others, when the wind whipped the broad, shallow steadies into whitecaps, many weeds were torn free from their moorings, and it was almost impossible to make a cast without picking up a piece of weed on the fly.

Because the river runs bank-full and is generally deep in flow, boats are used in many of the pools. On one such pool on the third beat, Heimir rowed me to an island from which I cast a fly he'd chosen, a Black Doctor, number eight, double, and hooked a salmon he estimated to weigh twenty-five pounds after the first leap and "maybe thirty" after the second. The fish, after a docile beginning, suddenly turned and headed seaward until half my backing was gone. The flow was smooth and steady, and I despaired of working him back to the tail of the island where we stood. Heimir, realizing this, went off to get the boat at the head of the island. By some miracle I did bring the fish up that hundred and fifty yards on our side of the lower island, only to have him dash through the deep, narrow cross-channel that separated us from the island below and led in a twisting course to the other main flow of the river and sweep downstream around the island's far side.

I held but the slightest tension and, helpless, watched the line go around rocks and branches at the stream's edge. Before my three hundred yards of backing ran out completely, Heimir came back with the boat and ferried me across the thirty feet of deep water to the tip of the lower island. I crashed my way along the shore, over rocks and through waist-high underbrush, clearing the line here and there where it twisted around a rock or a root, constantly wondering if the fish was still on and if all this exhausting effort was going to be worthwhile. Halfway down the lower island I found life at the end of the line and, again, the fish moved off downstream. I followed, moving unsteadily and clumsily in my waders over the difficult stream edge, wondering even more why I had to try so hard to save a fish I had almost no chance of saving anyway.

At the tail of that lower island the two main river currents joined with a rush and ran, white and forbidding, for a hundred yards. When Heimir, who had tied up the boat at the top of the island and taken a path down through it, finally found me, the salmon, which I'd worked back into fly-line range, started rolling over in the current and drifting farther downstream. Heimir went back for the boat.

By the time he returned I was holding a steady pressure on the backing, only fifty yards of which remained on the reel. We drifted down in the boat, freeing the line from a few rocks as we went along until it bent out into the current around a rock that threw white foam above it. Heimir turned into the current and rowed his best, but he couldn't enter the current near the rock and make any headway upstream. We eased closer to shore where the current was weaker and moved well upstream. Hard pulling failed to dislodge the line, and finally, even though I was sure the salmon was still on and resting in an eddy somewhere below us, I gave up and broke the line. Heimir and I waded the boat slowly back to the upper end of the island and crossed to the pool where the fish had risen, and where another salmon, a twelve-pounder, soon took my fly and came in without ever getting into my backing.

Heimir selected my flies most of the time, favoring the Black Doctor, Black Dose, Night Hawk and Jock Scott. Occasionally I surprised him. Once, when he sat at the rowing seat looking at his boot tips while I worked on a good salmon that was porpoising out in a smooth flow, I tied on a big, white, number 4 dry fly and started casting to the fish. As the fly's shadow crossed in front of him, Heimir's head jerked up. He saw the fly coming back on a false cast, and shouting "What's that!" ducked to the bottom of the boat. It was his first look at a big dry fly, and it shook him. Every time it came over, he ducked low, even though he'd been unconcerned when the double-hooked Jock Scott had been whistling by his ear.

"You'll never catch anything with a fly like that," he said, emphatically.

"The crazy salmon in Canada will take it," I countered.

"Maybe, but never one here," he said. And he was right. That particular salmon spurned not only the dry fly but all the wet flies I put over him as well.

Why is it one remembers the tough fish even more than the big ones? One evening when Heimir had taken Joan down to a pool that could only be fished from a boat, he directed me to a pool above where I could wade and reach much of the good water. It was blowing a living gale, right off the polar seas. (The Laxa flows north on Iceland's northwest coast.) I'd chosen my six-foot, 1⅝-ounce fiberglass rod for all my fishing, partly out of the pure pleasure of the light action and gentle touch and partly of cussedness because the local consensus was that it wasn't a suitable weapon for salmon.

The wind did cut something from the distance I could make with it on a calm day, but I felt I was covering a lot of good water. Not a salmon was showing—probably to keep from getting frostbitten, I thought.

An hour of fishing brought no action. The sun was low, and the quitting time of ten P.M., standard on most Icelandic rivers, was drawing near. I saw a salmon roll near the far bank, well beyond the casting range from the bar on which I waded. I went ashore and climbed aboard that pool's boat, rowed into the wind and anchored favorably to reach the fish. Two casts and he took the fly.

Rod in one hand, with the reel screaming, I tried to get the anchor up. It was stuck. Line was running out, deep into the backing. I tried harder, slowly lifting the anchor and a waterlogged stump it was caught in to the side of the boat. I couldn't lift it over the gunwale because of the rod in my hand that called (emphatically) for some gentle care. As the reel sang on, I threw caution to the winds and laid the butt of the rod over the rear seat with the reel hanging down to hold it in place. I knew a sudden spurt by the salmon might pop the reel up onto the seat and, from there, even a light pressure could pull it over the stern. I had to have two free hands for the anchor and even then it was a tough pull. By the time I'd lifted it and the stump up and disengaged the anchor, my line was near its end.

The wind blew me toward the fish so fast the line made a great bow in the water—and caught a snag. With both the rod and oar in my right hand I rowed back, drifted again, and caught another snag. Freeing the line from that one I caught still a third. Seeing bottom beneath me (Iceland's streams are beautifully clear), I threw out the anchor and slid overboard to wade. Afoot, I was able to free the line and work the fish in to a short line. Next he moved upstream into water I couldn't wade and picked up some weeds.

It was into the boat again, haul anchor and row upstream

till my breath was short; another bar and again the anchor went out. I went over the side once more to take up slack. The fish was still on! And he was tired. Hip deep, I drew him close for hand tailing, then waded to the boat and slid him in. It was ten minutes before my breathing was normal.

How big was he? Just nine pounds! Of all the salmon I caught in Iceland he made me work the hardest.



The Laxa is known as the queen of Iceland's rivers, with the biggest average for her salmon and the most uniform fishing conditions. Leaving it, to move on to the other rivers, we expected a let-down and said to ourselves, "I wish we could have saved this wonderful river till last."

## *The Nordura*

The Nordura in southwestern Iceland was next on our list. Instead of looking out on the gently rounded snow-capped mountains and the gentle slopes that stretched from one side of the Laxa valley to the other, at the Nordura we were surrounded by a wild mixture of twisting green meadows and raw volcanic rock. The stream bed looked as if a giant bulldozer had gouged its great channel, leaving splintered rocks in its wake that ranged from pebble size up to hundreds of tons. The river races through these rocky stretches and only occasionally meanders gently in a sweeping run or rests in a deep and quiet pool.

On reaching the lodge I was handed a note from C. W. Jacob, a companion of other days on many salmon rivers, who had been fishing there the previous week. "Great fishing!" he said. "Plenty of fish and they took our flies well." We read the note and nodded. Even then we were afraid it would be a letdown. We knew the fish would run smaller than those of the Laxa.

My first fish was a bright twelve-pounder. She used the fast flow to her advantage and, because I was back to my usual six-pound-test leader, she took me downstream two hundred yards to a quiet spot for the finale.

I'd expected her to be bigger because of the fierceness of her fight, but my eyes, at her leaps, had told me that twelve pounds would be about right. When she finally lay stretched out on the wet sands she was truly beautiful, the most shapely salmon I had seen since one that came my way on the Fox Island River in Newfoundland back in 1940. Small head, narrow tail stem, and between them a slim, smoothly streamlined body, silver-bright. She typified the best combination of power and speed. Traditionally, long slim fish are the toughest fighters.

Salmon vary in shape from river to river, and my fish was typical of the Nordura's fish. We came to love them for their flashing speed and their long runs. The river was higher than normal, and they used its twisting waters well in their flashing fights.

Most of the anglers of the Nordura fish with double-hooked flies, and the guides there, who were the finest group we'd seen on many a river, were convinced that we wouldn't hold many fish with our low-water-type single hooks.

I started out as a disbeliever but at the end of our four-day stay, I was more than half convinced. Normally, I fished a hitched or "skimming" wet fly, and I feel that the single-hooked flies skim more attractively than the doubles. The point of interest was that I did lose more fish than usual, and I found that most of my fish, instead of being hooked in the corner of the mouth as usual, were hooked in the forward part of the mouth where the hook's hold isn't as good. Being hooked near the nose, the salmon tended to fight with a lot of headshaking, feeling, perhaps, that they could shake off or rub off the fly.

A head-shaker is a difficult fish to play. Hold him tightly and he gets a lot of pressure on the line as he bends away. Hold him gently and he simply rests, and you get nowhere. If you're to tire him at all, you've got to put up with a lot of sharp tugs that will tear the hook free from the softer flesh of a fish's mouth more often than not. Double hooks under these conditions may hold better. If so, it will be the first time I've ever run into a river where this is true.



The Nordura salmon seem to be slow or late in deciding to take the fly and then suddenly eager to chase and catch it. Most of them take it from behind and just barely get it. I learned one thing fast: that was to leave my fly in the water if a fish rose and missed it. In most rivers a salmon will not leave his lie to chase a fly halfway across the river. They'll make one pass and that's all until the next cast or the tenth or the hundredth brings it close to them again. One out of every four salmon I hooked did the unusual and made a second or third *successful* attempt on the same cast.

I learned a special trick on the Nordura. With it I was able to hook some of the short risers. If a fish rose twice in the same place, chasing a little and missing, I'd concentrate on locating his rising spot. Once I'd located it, I'd abruptly slow the fly down just as he was due to rise. Three times on three salmon I'm sure I surprised not only myself but the fish with this ruse. The fish caught the slowed-down fly and were hooked as salmon should be: in the corner of the mouth. I wish I'd figured that trick out long before; perhaps I'd have hooked a lot of salmon that struck short a few times and then quit.

The Nordura, like the Laxa and all the other Icelandic rivers we fished, ran crystal-clear. When a salmon swirled at a fly, even though he was deep, his side became a flash of silver, and immediately you froze in your tracks and prepared to make identical casts to the same spot.

Joan and I had been enamoured of the Grastraumur pool on the Laxa. It was a pool to dream about that stretched from a rocky cliff down through a hundred yards of broad smooth flow that harbored a thousand salmon and gave them all the room they needed to play in. However, on our third day at the Nordura, Jonnas Halldorsson, our guide, took us to Stekkur, a long, deep and steady run that showed us more beauty and more beautiful action than any other pool of our trip.

The run was smooth with a gently sloping sheep pasture on the inner side of the crescent bend. It pressed against a high cliff of twisted, tortured bare volcanic rock. The flow was smooth, over a bed of mixed fine gravel and boulders. Wading to my wader tops, it took the best cast I could make to cover the deepest water on the far side. My flies skimmed smoothly, leaving a long "V" wake behind, and a salmon, in rising, showed his silver deep before he broke the surface with his jaws. Most of the fish we saw and caught were ten pounds or over.

Joan could fish through the central section and cover most of the fish. Coming behind her and wading more deeply and so casting farther out, I could reach the least-fished-for fish at maximum casting range. We caught five fish in our three-hour stay—and lost two others—and Joan, spotting a salmon lying abreast of her and thirty feet away, bedeviled him with a Royal Wulff dry fly until he made a pass at it—and missed.

## *The Haffjardara*

The Haffjardara belongs to a great blond viking named Thor Thors. He owns the farmland through which the river flows, and from the depths of his love for his land and the river, and for salmon fishing, he has kept it beautiful and full of fish. It is fished less than most rivers, and because of a growing abundance of salmon and greater competition on the spawning beds, he believes he is getting stronger, superior salmon.

We tend to agree. The fish averaged well in size and fought like demons. We watched them leaping a falls in midriver and marveled, as always, at the stored-up energy and concentrated power these fish possess.

On the Haffjardara I ran a test of dry fly versus wet; a fair test. Admittedly the river was a trifle high but not far above normal. The day was a pleasant one with the temperature hanging around seventy. The water at that pool was slow and steady, pressing against an undercut bank in a meadow.

I put on a number 8 Royal and drifted it carefully over the stretch of water my guide, Diddi, had assured me held a number of salmon. I made a hundred casts. Nothing stirred!

Changing to a hitched wet fly I fished back downstream over the same water *and hooked three salmon.*

On a good day, giving the dry fly first opportunity, it failed to produce. Admittedly, salmon have been taken on a dry fly in Iceland, but this indicated to me that a wet fly is far, far more effective under most conditions. True, a skimmed wet fly is awfully close to a dry fly in many ways, but those Icelandic fish had a preference for a moving fly at, or under, the surface level, and they showed it!



## *The Grimsa*

The Grimsa was the last of our rivers. The president of the Reykjavik Salmon Angling Club, who had dropped in at the Nordura, during our stay, for an afternoon of fishing and had promptly caught the biggest fish of the week, a twenty-one-pounder, had called the Grimsa the best river in Iceland. We wondered how it would compare with the others.

It is a longer river than most, with salmon running more than forty miles inland. It flows through a soft landscape made up of seemingly endless farms. The pools are for the most part gravel-bottomed, typical of meadow streams, except for a mile or so where the river flows through a ledgy rock channel and over a falls that forces the salmon to take valiantly to the air. Its fish run anywhere from three to thirty pounds with a good share well over twenty. It seemed to us to be well filled with salmon, and we saw many twenty-plus pounders though we never did catch one.

In Iceland the rivers are divided into "beats" and each beat is designed to produce for its anglers from 1200 to 1500 fish during the season. The pools were heavy with fish, and one could imagine being able to hook a dozen salmon in a fifty-foot stretch of stream. But the Grimsa fish were very particular in their choice of flies and presentations. They wanted a fly of a particular size and one that moved in a certain way.

Here again, in a good stretch of river I tried a dry fly, this time a skater. I danced it across the water in the afternoon sun; water that had been rested since the day before. Again the air was warm, and the wind was light. For a hundred feet, nothing stirred under my fly, though I kept expecting action at every cast.

Changing to a skimmed number six Haggis, I covered the same water with casts of similar length and swing. Just as on the Haffjardara, three salmon rose and were hooked and landed from the same stretch in half the fishing time. The dry fly obviously does not have the same charm for Icelandic fish that it does for Canadian salmon.

The Grimsa was a challenging river throughout its length. Late-entering August fish carrying sea lice were mixed in with dark-gray old-timers of the June run. It was here that Joan really became a knowing salmon angler.

During several fishing periods I had taken fish where she had gone without a rise. She had asked me what she must do to catch fish as consistently as I did.

It's hard to explain why one angler fishing a salmon pool catches fish while another on the same or similar water doesn't get a rise. I think it is some special movement of the fly as it swims or drifts—something special imparted to it that affects the salmon. Words cannot explain this phenomenon easily because

it varies with each salmon lie and each speed of water, with each varying eddy. So I asked Joan to stop fishing and watch my fly to see if she could see any difference between her retrieves and mine. I believe the secret of drawing rises lies in the fly's approach to, and passage by, the salmon. It requires an intentness most anglers fail to give, a picturing of a salmon lying in wait and the bending, speeding or slowing down of the retrieve to make the fly most tantalizing. If an angler gets a feeling a spot is particularly hot, he'll make three or four casts there instead of just one before moving on downstream with his coverage, varying those casts just a little, searching for the perfect movement. It takes experience for an angler to know the retrieve that is "right" for any particular water, but it will usually be close to the speed of fly that has taken salmon before, pretty much across the current and slightly upstream from the fish.

Whether it was the periods of watching she put in or some special thought she gave to her fly's movements, from that time on, her take improved. On the Grimsa, on several occasions she took more or bigger fish than I, and I know that now she has the "feel" of salmon fishing just as a good pilot gets the feel of flying.

I had been taking pride in a record of catching at least one salmon in every morning or afternoon period of our fishing in Iceland. "Consistency," I thought, is the prime virtue, the ability to penetrate their defenses no matter how hot and bright or how cold and windy the day, how high or low the water.

On the last evening we fished a run of medium speed and shallow depth, water in which I thought salmon should rise well. When we reached the pool and saw salmon jumping regularly throughout a hundred-yard stretch, we expected to go out in a blaze of glory. This pool had been dry for ten years because of a change of course of the river, and only because of a low earth dam across the new course had it been forced back into its old bed. A few big rocks broke the flow here and there; lesser rocks made ideal salmon lies throughout its length.

Starting at five, we had five hours to fish. It should have been a cinch. But the hours went by and no matter how diligently we fished, working over fish we knew were lying just a few feet under the flies we cast, not one salmon moved to take our flies.

The sun fell low in the sky, and the chill of evening closed in on our frustration. Time after time I'd moved through the fast water at the head of the pool, fished the middle section where most of the fish were jumping and wound up at the slow, steady run at the tail. In desperation I tried very small flies and, finally, larger ones.

Eventually I put on a fly I'd picked up in Scotland years before as a souvenir because it looked so unlikely to take a salmon. It was a fly of Jock Scott characteristics tied on a three-inch twisted wire shank with a number six treble trailing behind. (Treble hooks are legal in Iceland and the European salmon waters.) It was a fly for major floods when lots of branches and debris are floating down the river. Joan laughed as I tied it on, and I smiled ruefully, thinking: This is the crowning absurdity where a usually knowing angler looks helplessly at his flies and doesn't know which way to turn.

Three casts and a salmon hit it. Five minutes later, with the leader well into the guides, he calmly opened his mouth to yawn and the monstrous fly came free. I continued to cast that monstrosity for another ten minutes, awkward as that casting was with my delicate six-foot rod. Finally I gave up and returned to the most successful patterns we'd used: Haggis, Lady Joan, Jock Scott, Blue Charm and Black Doctor. Once I thought I saw a swirl where a salmon made a soggy rise below the fly, but I saw no flash of silver, although I cast intently to that spot from nine-forty-five till ten, with fish jumping above, below and beside my fly. None came to touch the hook. Finally, in my last evening of fifteen days of fishing, I was skunked. A fitting rebuff by an unpredictable fish to an angler who was growing to think he could *always* fool them.

In Iceland the Atlantic salmon are well managed and on the increase. Practically all netting has been eliminated, and the salmon is, in essence, a game fish. The harvest is by angling, and there are no daily or weekly limits and no need for them, for limiting the number of anglers automatically limits the harvest sufficiently. With the salmon increasing, one can be sure the take is not too heavy. (Salmon are rarely released in Iceland, because there is no overfishing, but we released over twenty on the Grimsa.) Just as the farmer-owners are paid for the right to fish the river, the anglers may keep or sell their fish if they wish.

Now that the angling world has discovered the Iceland salmon fishing, the last and only well-managed haven of all, the pressure to fish there is great and growing. I think the Icelandic government will have to step in and decree that a certain percentage of the fishing days must be reserved for Icelanders at a moderate fee, to ensure their opportunity to participate in this magnificent fishing, and that the balance will be sold on the open market at whatever price the nonresident anglers will pay. Rates on the major rivers at present range from $1500 to $1800 per angler per week. I think that figure is sure to double in the next few years. Overpriced? Nothing is overpriced when there's a line-up waiting to buy it.

Iceland has solved the Atlantic salmon problem, increasing their runs to full river capacity while drawing a maximum return in dollars and sport for a sensible harvest. The world can well take heed to study and perhaps adapt their salmon angling systems, whether private or public. For us it would mean the sort of restrictions Colorado now puts on its limited and valuable bighorn sheep.

*Tally for 15 Days of Fishing*

| | | | |
|---|---|---|---|
| Laxa Adaldal | 4 days | Joan 3 | Lee 9 |
| Nordura | 4 days | Joan 9 | Lee 20 |
| Haffjardara | 1 day | Joan 1 | Lee 5 |
| Grimsa | 6 days | Joan 11 | Lee 35 |
| Total | 15 days | 93 fish | |

# I Remember Cuba

GRITS GRESHAM



Ceferino Valero gave one more dig with the paddle, then let the heavy wooden boat mush to a halt. When I twisted toward him from my bow seat the seventeen-year-old guide flashed a toothy grin, gestured toward the open water of the lake, and said, *"Pescar."*

Fish here? In the middle of the lake? I looked longingly toward the distant shoreline which was rimmed with fishy-looking weed cover, but dutifully I picked up my rod and made a cast.

The Swimming Minnow splashed down at random because one patch of water seemed just as uninspiring as any other, and I began a routine retrieve. Underwater weeds grabbed the hooks and got my attention, briefly, but then the lifeless feel told me that this was no fish. This was, after all, what I expected.

On the second cast I kept the lure from sinking quite as deep by beginning the retrieve as soon as the plug hit the water, and by keeping the rod tip high. But again, after a few cranks on the reel, I felt something. And, again from instinct and habit, I struck back and felt the hooks go home in a good fish.

The seven-pound largemouth jumped twice, dove deep to tangle briefly in the submerged moss, but finally rolled over at boatside. Ceferino's grin was a bit wider when I grabbed the bass by the jaw and swung him aboard, as if to say, "Not bad for openers, eh?"

Howard Rivers leaned into his push-pole to send our skiff zipping across the shallow flats on an interception course with the school of feeding bonefish. Just out of casting range he shipped the pole and let us drift in.

I crouched low in the bow, presenting as little silhouette as possible to the spooky fish, as the boat and the tailing bones converged on each other. There! One fish, ahead of the school, was in range.

With a flip of the spinning rod I dropped the crab-baited hook a few feet in front of the bonefish, engaged the bail, cranked the handle three or four times, and waited. The fish picked up the crab in no-nonsense fashion and blazed away in its inimitable fashion when I raised the rod tip sharply.

With rod held high to keep the monofilament from scraping bottom, I thrilled to the mad dash of a typically strong bonefish. Then the song of the reel drag settled to a lower pitch as the fish tired and began to circle, but suddenly the line went limp.

"No set hook!" an unsmiling Howard Rivers pronounced after I had reeled back in. He jammed the push-pole into the bottom and continued our cruise along the mangrove-fringed island. Ten minutes later he pointed with the pole, without speaking, to more bonefish.

Same song, second verse; but this time, when the fish picked up the crab, Howard's accusing words were fresh in my mind, and I rocked back on the rod with authority. And again the bonefish sped away in that slashing run.

*"SET DE HOOK!"* came the stern warning from my guide before the fish had gone twenty-five yards. I dutifully popped it to him one more time, this time with enthusiasm which shook the skiff.

*"SET DE HOOK!!"* screamed Howard as the bonefish passed the fifty-yard mark with no deviation in either course or speed. This time, fearing that I might have to walk back to camp, I got with the program. With a mighty sweep I socked it to the fish—breaking the line.

"Too hard." The philosophical guide shrugged and, still unsmiling, returned to his poling.

Bill Mas Sarda watched with obvious approval as his eight-year-old son played give-and-take with the big barracuda. With clenched teeth the stocky youngster hung on with both hands as the strong fish ripped line from the reel, and between each slashing run his pump-and-reel technique flirted with the expert.

Earlier that day we had enjoyed seeing the boy whip a forty-pounder, and this 'cuda was bigger—much bigger. The fish had taken a bait on one of our flat lines, close in, sailing high out of the water at the strike in a manner reminiscent of kingfish or bull dolphin. The show-off maneuver did just that: revealed the barracuda as the monster it was.

The strike of the biggest fish of the day, typically enough, was on our lightest tackle. The pairing would have been more even had it been on one of the heavier outrigger lines, which danced skipping baits over the waves in search of marlin.

But the deed was done and little Billy, with twenty-pound-test to work with, had to play the 'cuda's game. It was a tune of give a lot and retrieve a little for the first half-hour, but the sweat-soaked youngster shook off any suggestion of help. Then the tide of battle swung our way, rapidly, with the runs becoming fewer and shorter.

After that the end came quickly. Sensing victory, Billy put more muscle into the rod, then moved from the fighting chair to the rail when the mate grabbed the leader and reached over with the gaff.

The great fish was whipped, on its side, cavernous tooth-filled jaws opened wide. Then, just out of range of the gaff, the barracuda flipped his head one more time, and it was the final straw. The leader, probably kinked at some time during the fight, parted, and as we watched in disbelief the huge fish slowly sank from sight.

For seconds all eyes focused on a disappointed eight-year-old. Then Bill Mas Sarda clapped his son on the shoulder, nodded a quick "Well done," and signaled the captain to move on.

Ben Calloway leaned his two hundred pounds into a two-handed cast, firing the spoon far out toward the hulk of a burned-out ship. The lure splashed down among the school of rolling tarpon, and before it could sink a fish took it.

"Look at that!" Ben shouted, to nobody in particular, as the ten-pounder cleared water in typical tarpon fashion. At the height of the gill-rattling jump the spoon sailed free, but no matter. Another fish was on before the angler could begin a retrieve.

Except for me, behind my camera, nobody else on the boat was paying any attention to Ben's action—because all of them also had tarpon hooked. We had been in the school of baby fish for about an hour, having super fun on light tackle.

I ran off the rest of the shots on the Rollei and returned to my casting rod. Minutes later a scene being played on the shore of the bay, a hundred yards from our boat, got our attention. The attention rapidly turned to fright!

Three army trucks roared down to the water's edge, skidding to a halt in a cloud of dust. From them poured men in uniform carrying rifles and machine guns—all of them leveled in our direction.

For this was Cuba, in 1960, the year One A.C.—After Castro.

Pearl of the Antilles! Cuba is indeed a jewel of an island. Discovered by Columbus in 1492, it is the largest isle in the West Indies. Only ninety miles south of Key West, Florida, it is flanked on the west by the Gulf of Mexico and on the south by the Caribbean.

It is surrounded, on all sides, by fish!

Sport fishing along the entire 730-mile length of the main island and around the offshore islands is excellent. And in the interior, in the Zapata Swamp, live the biggest largemouth bass in the world.

Point of order! Sport fishing *was* good and the big bass *did* live, a dozen years ago. What has happened since then? Nobody in the U.S.A. knows because we were the last anglers from this country to fish in Cuba.

That trip was my one and only trip to Cuba; and before I had been in Havana twenty-four hours, I was infatuated with the country. Tradition and antiquity turn me on, and this capital city had both in quantity: ancient buildings with character, broad streets laced with many inviting parks, delicious coffee available at sidewalk stands in every block.

And Cubans; as a people they are warm, friendly, and outgoing. And, when I was there they were happy, for that was a period of transition—from frying pan to fire!

Two weeks of fishing, from the Isle of Pines to the Zapata Swamp to the bay at Havana, turned my infatuation into a full-blown love affair. "Pearl of the Antilles" is a superbly appropriate name. Cuba is a beautiful place with a diversity unique to tropical islands. It has miles and miles of splendid beaches bordering on the crystal-clear waters of the Gulf and the Caribbean, and it has the bewildering and productive Zapata Swamp.

And Cuba has mountains, both in the east and the west, with the highest peak soaring to 6467 feet. That's about the same as the highest mountain in eastern North America.

I fished Treasure Lake, in the Zapata Swamp, late one Saturday afternoon for about two hours and again the next morning for the same length of time. It was like opening the door to the mother lode but just opening it a crack.

Ceferino was pleased with my first bass, but that seven-pounder turned out to be my biggest in the four hours of fishing, most of it in the rain. Fishing with me in the boat, Ben Calloway hooked and lost two keepers which we guesstimated at twelve to fourteen pounds.

I captured one of Ben's biggies on film before it ripped free of the hooks, and he now looks down on me from the wall of my den. The fish is so awesome, completely clear of the water with gills open wide, that few viewers recognize it as a freshwater bass.

Ofelio Rodriguez operated the boat landing from which we fished Treasure Lake, and part of the operation was a small cantina featuring an open-air, thatched-roof dance floor. As we drove down the rough, muddy road toward the lake late Saturday afternoon we passed dozens of Cubans headed the same way; some were in wagons, but most came on foot. From five miles away and more, they were headed for the Saturday-night dance at Rodriguez Landing.

When we returned down that same road at dawn the next morning, we met that same stream of people. They were returning home following a full night of merry-making, and that is typical of these fun-loving people.

While fishing Treasure Lake we stayed in the city of Cienfuegas, a striking port on the southern coast of Cuba. It was carnival time, and the Hotel Jagua—a simply magnificent hotel overlooking the spectacular harbor—was a festive place.

Bonefish, snook, and tarpon fishing were excellent around Cienfuegas at the time. Now, a dozen years later, I wonder how well they've competed with the submarines.

Several years before my trip a friend of mine caught a bass from Treasure Lake which weighed more than seventeen pounds. Eddie Woods, noted exhibition caster and angler, admitted that his catch was a good fish. But, he added, when he played the fish to the boat a second bass, a really big one, was trying to get the lure. Eddie wasn't kidding.

Reports persist that thirty-pound bass have been speared by Cuban commercial fishermen. Viva Zapata Swamp!

The Isle of Pines. It was there, while fishing out of the camp of Vic Barothy, who pioneered and popularized light-tackle fishing in Cuba, that guide Howard Rivers provided one of the funniest angling episodes of my life. His "Too hard!" when I popped the line while following his urgings to set the hook was almost too much. I didn't quite fall out of the skiff from laughter, but almost, and even Howard finally grinned a bit.

The miles and miles of great bonefish flats in that area haven't been touched by fishermen. And tarpon? At times you could almost catch them from the porch of Vic's cabin.

Offshore—marlin, barracuda, bonita, shark; around the entire 2500 mile shoreline of Cuba the fishing was excellent. Two years before I talked with him, and fished with him, Julio Garrido caught a blue marlin, on a hand line, which weighed 1100 pounds.



Frank Bowery, from Cayman Island, catching eight hundred to a thousand sharks per year, selling the hides, fins and liver . . . The beautiful Columbus Cathedral, in Havana, which was built about the same time the Pilgrims landed in Massachusetts . . . Lunch in the Hotel Gran Paris in Matanzas. Superior. Choose your own live langostino (river shrimp) from the pool in the courtyard . . . Bill Mas Sarda, our official government guide for the two-week stay in Cuba, suffering in silence for days as I told of my prowess with the shotgun as well as the fishing rod, then finally admitting that he did indeed win the world live pigeon championship in Portugal in 1957, with 38x38.



The soldiers, obviously, didn't open up with their automatic weapons when we were fishing tarpon in the bay at Havana, but we had some anxious moments. We were there with the blessing of Premier Castro. He knew that, and we knew that; but did the officer in charge of that collection of bearded, machine-gun-equipped youngsters know that? An explanation after the fact would have been small consolation!

Bill Mas Sarda's gestures and shouts were in time to identify us as the harmless fishermen we were. It seems that we had been fishing for two hours in a sensitive area—the spot where a munitions ship had exploded and burned a short time earlier—and it made the natives restless.

I was invited back to Cuba later that year. But by then Bill Mas Sarda had fled to this country, and I allowed the realization that I had been an awfully hard boy to raise to overcome my crush on the Pearl of the Antilles.

Each day the huge bass looks down from the photograph on my wall.

And I remember the Pearl . . . and grieve.

# The North and the South of It

HOMER CIRCLE



Punching the memory key and setting one's brain to the task of sorting through forty-six years of kaleidoscopic flashbacks of fishing experiences over four continents is, indeed, a challenging mental exercise. I am unable to eliminate either of two unlike, unforgettable moments of truth. So I'll tell you about both.

First, let me explain myself to those who know me not. I am one of the world's luckiest guys. As angling editor of *Sports Afield,* I get paid to fish; writing about it is a fringe benefit. Also, I'm

blessed with a wife who lives to fish, my childbride of some thirty-six years, Gayle, and I have watched admiringly as she's toughed it out from the frigid Arctic to the steaming jungles to experience the challenges and the joys of fishing.

One trip involved a far-north jaunt to the Inman River, which flows into the Arctic Ocean in Canada's Northwest Territories. Our float plane circled the mouth of the river, the pilot carefully assessing slots among the icebergs floating in the area.

We scudded to an aquatic landing and taxied up the Inman to a gravel bar, where we climbed out and started assembling our tackle. Our companions were another couple, Frank and Pat Carter, enthusiastic anglers who share our junkets where adventure beckons.

The fishing at the river outlet served to lower our fishing fever with smaller Arctic char, the fish we had come over three thousand miles to catch.

"Upriver by the big bluff hole is where the whoppers dwell," advised our guide. "And it's quite a haul, so we better start trekking because according to our forecast there might be a bit of weather moving in."

So, we grabbed gear and began trekking, and what a wild and desolate kind of beauty we saw. Despite the fact that the permanent frost line was only a few feet below the earth's surface, wildflowers grew in profusion. One flower seemed especially appropriate for the Arctic, a short plant with snowy white blossoms that dotted the landscape like tiny rabbit tails afluff in the ground breeze.

There were no trees because we were about 185 miles north of the tree line. On our way upriver we ran across a native "freezer," a shaft dug into the ground, just large enough for a man to crawl into. At the bottom were several barrels of oil, probably seal oil, in which were stored chunks of meat. The interior of the shaft was ice-walled, and many caribou hams were suspended there, preserved in this "deep freeze." Typical of the life in this remote area was a note from an Eskimo trapper to his Canadian friend who also trapped for a part of his living. It was written on a slab of fiber board from a nearby crude shelter. It read:

Dear Friend:

You should of been here about a week ago. You should of

seen caribow all over the place. You would of got lots of caribow for the winter. We started from Paulatuk on Nov. 1.

*(Signed)* Jonah Makemayak

P.S. We took two hams of caribow from the deep freeze because we had no more dog food. And some fish, about 20. Thank you.



Obviously, in this barren country it's a case of share and survive, and I'm sure the Eskimo repaid the favor in the simple, trustworthy manner common to most natives of the north country.

We hiked up and down hills to reach the big bluff hole, and it was a beaut. Clean, cold, pure, undefiled water pouring abundantly into a deep, dark hole where there just had to be jumbo Arctic char. Our challenge was to find what would tempt the bigger, wiser denizens.

Each angler began his traditional, instinctive search through lures that had come through on other species of fish similar to the char. This meant spinners, spoons, streamers, and other trout tempters that worked on rainbows, browns, brooks, and lake trout in other places. Although we caught several dozen smaller char on most any lure we used, the larger ones in the ten-pound-and-up class proved elusive. We finally hit on a combination of lures that had enough weight to sink fast, and with a steep angle of dive that kept them grubbing the rocky bottom on the retrieve.

We had a ball vying for the largest fish, each trying to conceal his secret "killer" and yet knowing, from brief glimpses of lures flashing through the air, what each was using. We must have landed and released unharmed upward of two dozen beautiful, silvery char. We kept only a half dozen to take back for eating, for photographs to grace our memory file, and for story needs. During all this activity, we had been laughing, bantering, shouting back and forth, and just having an enthusiastically good time, aware that our voices were echoing off the bluff walls.

Suddenly, amidst all our jollity, Frank's eyes swept skyward and he gave out with an awed whisper: "Talk about an unforgettable sight. Will y'all look at that majestic bull caribou?"

We looked, and there atop the bluff that towered over us stood a monarch of this frozen tundra country, gazing down on us. His contained, regal bearing and a toss of his huge rack told us more eloquently than words that we were intruders in his domain.

The only audible sound as we exchanged glances was the burbling of the water over boulders, and our measured breathing, almost in involuntary deference to this lordly reindeer. Slowly, his head lowered as his eyes seemed to appraise each of us. Then, seemingly reassured that we represented no threat, he raised high his trophy rack, turned away, and after one final rearward glance, disappeared from view. It was a sobering, fulfilling experience, and we all felt privileged to have had it. The caribou obviously was in his prime, and we conjectured as to how he existed in this barren countryside. Migration had to be the answer, because forage was getting mighty slim at that time of year.

When we departed, the pilot flew a search pattern, and we spotted him in a valley, alone, making his way southward. We swung low over him, and he favored us with one tolerant glance as he continued his journey. We saluted him, and we were thankful we had been privileged to cross trails with such a grand creature. It was the icing on the cake, a capper to a fishing experience par excellence. And we shall never forget it!

Now my mind flashes over thousands more miles, southward to Ecuador where I had heard about some giant, hybrid trout high in the Andes. It wouldn't be an easy trip; in fact, I was informed it would be on the rugged side. On my job this simply means there's an unusual story to be done.

While jetting to Quito in the competent hands of Braniff Airlines (who were sending us there to check out the possibilities of this hybrid hotspot for possible inclusion in their outdoor trip book), we laid plans for our campaign.

My compadre was Wally Taber, well known for his top flight travelogues of adventure in far-out places. Our guide, Colonel Sam Hogan, had appraised us of our needs, and his admonition was, "Travel light, because every pound can feel like twenty-five before the day is over!"

We knew that our hybrid fish was a rainbow-cutthroat trout which Uncle Sam had furnished to Ecuador. That country's fisheries department had planted them via airplane in ten high-mountain lakes. Colonel Sam had sampled most of them and we were going to his pick of the lot, Lago Penas Blancas, "lake of the white rocks."

"From what I got from the Colonel's letter, we are in for an unusual trip," Wally grinned in anticipation. "Well, I brought plenty of film and plenty of candy bars for energy."

That night at Colonel Sam's hacienda we sat down for a briefing.

"We're going for the high one where the hybrids average six to ten pounds and leap higher than any freshwater fish you ever saw. I hope you two have your lungs and muscles in fine fettle," Sam told us.

Sam, at fifty-six, had recently retired from our military at the American embassy in Quito. He was tall, trim, and hard as an oak stump. But, at his same approximate age, Wally and I kept in above-average physical shape, and we weren't too concerned about the workout.

"Lago Penas Blancas is an incredibly beautiful lake," Sam informed us. "And it's almost three miles upstairs. We can drive all but the last mile. It's a steep climb up and a steeper climb going down.

"Then, when you finally look down on this shimmering beauty, you're standing on the edge of a cliff several hundred feet high. You'll swear we've come all this way for nothing. Then, you won't believe it when you see it. The way down. I promise you it's something neither of you has experienced before. Unique!"

He let us sleep on that. At daybreak he routed us out, fed us bountifully, and we were upward bound by sunrise. We climbed upward through the clouds, stopped at the base of a lofty ridge, and unloaded the Land Rover.

Each of us carried his own gear. In my case it was a pair of waders forked over my neck, camera bag, fishing rods, lure satchel, and a foul-weather suit. Wally was equally laden.

The smallish Indian guides carried ponchos on their backs, suspended by head straps. They carried cooking utensils, more of Wally's movie equipment, lunch fixings, etc., but they never slowed down as they moved upward.

The grade was so steep we had to hold onto tufts of dry grass to keep from sliding backward at times. We wended our way back and forth, pausing every dozen steps to gasp for air and wait for a pounding heart to slow to a tolerable rate.

Laboriously, and after what seemed an eternity of little

agonies, we reached the summit of the ridge. Then, we saw it. Lago Penas Blancas; deep blue water formed an elongate gut with shiny white rocks bordering the shoreline. As Sam said, incredibly beautiful.

"Ready to go the last mile?" Sam grinned. "The best part is just ahead."

I thought he meant the fishing, but the canny Colonel had another surprise in mind.

We crept and slid downward until we reached the rim of a precipice. Two hundred feet straight down looked like the end of the trail.

"How do we get down?" we asked in unison.

Sam made a one-sided grin and pointed to the top of a tree jutting about three feet above the rim of the sheer rocky wall.

"There, gentlemen, is our way down. It saves a two-day horse ride up the valley. After you make it once, you learn to like it," he encouraged.

We watched the two guides go first. They made it look simple. They held onto a tuft of grass with one hand, grabbed the tree top with the other, released the grass, grasped the tree with both hands and stayed with it until it stopped swaying. Then they climbed down.

As Sam had said, here was something we hadn't experienced before. I was next, ol' lucky Homer. When I made my grab for that tree I think it was a new experience for the tree, too. Never before had it been subjected to such a death grip!

It swayed away from the cliff, and I hung on until it steadied. When I reached the bottom, I looked up to see what we had climbed down. The tree grew out of the top of a hundred-foot mound, and this explained how its tip reached the rim of the precipice.

This surely beats a two-day horseback ride, I kept telling myself. But I wasn't sure I believed me.

We worked our way down to the lake, rigged fishing gear and cameras, and began the wildest six-hour fishing stint I've ever experienced.

First, the sun would shine warmly and beautifully. Then it would cloud up and alternately dump rain, sleet, and snow on us. Raw cold numbed our hands. Back would come the sun, and we'd hurry to shoot our pictures because we knew the rain, sleet, and snow weren't far behind.

Those hybrids proved to be everything Sam had said they

were: big, strong, long on the fight, and crazy high jumpers. Both Wally and I got some great shots of the action, and we were feeling that great feeling of knowing we had a winner going.

Yet, in each of our minds lurked an irksome thought. Our eyes would occasionally take a fleeting glance at that cotton-pickin' tree. It was impossible not to think about the climb back up that giant and wonder how we were going to make it back onto that precarious mountainside. No one mentioned it, but we all thought about it.

The period of pleasure came to an end, and the moment of truth faced us. We kept only six of several dozen trout we had caught, because we knew every pound had to be carried, the hardest way. This, my friend, will make a rabid conservationist of the greediest fisherman!

The two diminutive guides divided the load of fish between them, and they climbed the tree first. When each reached the top, he started the tree swaying, held onto it with one hand, and reached out toward the mountainside with the other. As the tree swayed inward he suddenly leaped, grabbed a handful of tufted grass, and held on, *grinning.*

"Nothing to it," said Colonel Sam. "Only he'll be there to give you a hand when you're ready to give it a go."

And that's precisely what he did. When I swayed the tree top toward him, careful not to look down, he suddenly reached out to grasp my forearm and literally snatched me out of that tree onto the mountainside. I think I grabbed everything grabbable and held on.

It was an experience I'll remember in every detail so long as I live. It had agonies, ecstacies, thrills, chills, and left me with a feeling of having done something beyond the call of duty.

The tall tree and the bull caribou; each a symbol in its own way. Each spelling out a simple truth. An outdoor man must get lost once in a while, if only to find himself. And these are the places where it happens!

# Reminiscence Provoked

PAT SMITH



Somehow I can't get a handle on this story.

It's probably my fault. I never was very adept at what Professor Middendorf called "expository narrative" back when Columbia was accepting non-radicals like me. Just give me a little action, like a big bass at dawn or a broadbill jumping black against the sky, and I can go pretty good—but ask me a silly question like why I love fishing and I'm up against the wall. What's scary is that I *know* that the Schwieberts, Underwoods

and Lyonses are going to take off on this and come up with very fine, highly readable answers—and that I'm going to appear stupid by comparison.

Somehow it seems unfair as hell. But then, fairness has never been the strong suit of a successful publisher or editor. Nor, for that matter, has compassion, humility, tenderness, generosity (in any form) or a common sense of decency. In fact the only thing common to the entire lot is a very broad, black, cruel streak of deviousness based on the premise that all writers are mental laggards who must be pushed to produce anything significant. What really hurts is: They're right.

So, with full malice aforethought, the devious partnership of James Rikhoff and Eric Peper has, by posing the question, pushed this writer to his outer limits—a particularly unsettling terrain for an individual who with each passing season aspires more and more to Harris tweeds, old brandy, blazing firesides and all the other traditional trappings of a clean, well-lighted life.

But tradition won't help me now. Here I stand, naked and without a compass, on this frozen, roadless plain with nothing going for me but a fuzzy memory and the dim hope of an empathetic reader or two. Somehow I've got to find my way back to that blazing fireside, where Rikhoff and Peper are warming themselves at this very moment. So, here goes.

THE WRITER: How did this all-consuming affair with fishing begin? Was it love at first sight?

THE SELF: How the hell do I know?

W: Come on, Try!

S Well, let's see. I can remember a day when I was about six. School had been let out for the summer and a kid named Altie Morgan and I went fishing for killies in the East Bronx where we lived. But you don't want to hear about that. . . .

W: Yes, I do. Go on. Where did you get the tackle—the rods and lines and everything?

S: We "borrowed" them from my father. He had a couple of casting rods, so we just sort of . . . took them. You know?

S: Yeah, I know. You mean you swiped them, right?

S: Uh, yeah. I guess you could say that if you wanted to be technical. Anyway, we used tiny hooks, number 20 or 22, and we baited them with little bread balls and —

w: Exactly where did you fish?

s: It was a little outlet along the Hutchinson River Parkway.

w: What kind of an outlet?

s: Ah, knock it off! You know as well as I that it was a rotten sewage outlet. So what if it wasn't the Madision or the Snake! The Bronx isn't exactly a natural paradise, you know!

w: Look, I'm just trying to help you remember accurately. I don't like it out on this God-forsaken wasteland either; so the sooner you get with it, the sooner we'll be back sipping brandy by that fireside.

s: Yeah, you're right. But, the fact is, this particular fishing experience is still slightly painful for me.

w: Why?

s: Well, because we kept catching killies, and we didn't notice how dark it was getting. The next thing I remember is the patrol car pulling up, and this giant cop asking me my name. The cops took us home, and there they were, my mother and father—waiting. My father was just happy to get his rods back intact. But my mother, she really laid into me. I think I bawled for several weeks. But now that I look back on it, I'm sure that my mother wasn't so mad about my staying out after dark as she was about other things. My report card, for instance . . .

w: Were you a poor student?

s: Yeah . . . I don't know why exactly. Hey, wait a minute! Let's stick to fishing! You're making sounds like a shrink.

w: You don't have to talk about it if you don't want to.

s: You're damn right I don't! Anyway, this isn't getting us anywhere. I'd have to be some kind of weirdo to love fishing because of that experience. Let's start over again.

w: All right. But hurry up! I'm getting cold.

s: Okay, but this isn't easy, you know. All that winter my parents worried about me growing up in the city. So the next summer we went out to Wisconsin.

w: It was the summer of '44?

s: Right. That's Where my father was "born and bred," as he put it. We rented a little cottage on Sturgeon Bay, complete with a small, plywood rowboat with a 3.3-horse outboard. God, how I loved it out there; clean water, big, wide sky and all the room any kid could handle. That very first day my father, my grandfather and I went fishing for bass. The wind was kicking up, and I guess I was more than a little afraid. But my grandfather just reached over and put his arm around me and told me not to worry. And you know something? I stopped worrying, and I've never been afraid of rough weather since. It was something about the way he talked; the way he could laugh at almost anything. Nothing fazed him. He could shrug, close his eyes, smile and laugh all at once. He was just a big, sweet, safe man . . . and I believed in him very much.

W: Go on, go on.

S: Well, that's the way it went all that first month. We fished every day, even in the rain; just the three of us, three pals. There wasn't a hint of a generation gap. Every July after that we would rent that same cottage, but the fishing was only part of it. You see, my father worked nights a lot as a rewrite man for the *The Daily News* in New York. He loved his job—and the people in it—so much that . . . well, I hardly ever saw him. But out in Wisconsin we were always together. My grandmother called me Shadow, because wherever my father and grandfather went, I went. Then came that summer when my father got sick . . . remember?

W: Yeah, I remember. It was 1950. We were thirteen. You want me to tell it?

S: No, damnit! This is one story you're not going to ruin by couching it in phony language. No, *I'm* telling this one *my* way. After the ambulance left, I ran into my room and curled up on the bed. I was shaking and sobbing from way down inside my guts. Then I felt my grandfather's big hand on my back, and I'll never forget what he said. "Pat," he said, "You must stop crying. Because if you don't, I'm going to cry too. So please help me." I looked up into that big, strong face and said, "Let's go fishing." And so we did. It was a flat calm as we pushed off and headed for a favorite spot called "The Wreck," a tangle of submerged timbers from a barge that went down about the turn of the century. We fished in silence for quite a while, until a neighbor came skipping out in a high-powered outboard and told us that my father had been operated on and that it looked like he would make it. Then my grandfather began to cry, and now it was my turn to reach out and put my arm around him as he did that first day when the wind was kicking up. You see, my father was what *connected* my grandfather and me. He was sort of the medium for our love. And fishing, I guess, was the thing that strung us all together.

w: Why do you remember that year so much?

s: Well, I suppose it's because the good times sort of took care of themselves, and they merged in my memory so that I can't really distinguish one from another. Another reason is that my father's sudden illness threatened that beautiful, generational relationship we had going from one year into the next. When something as deep as that is threatened, you remember. You never forget.

w: What else do you remember? Keep going, we're making progress now. I think I see a cabin up ahead.

s: Well, unfortunately, I had to grow up. I joined the Marines right out of high school and—

w: Why didn't you go on to college?

s: Look, goddammit! I already told you I was a lousy student, so let's drop it, okay?

w: If you wish.

s: I wish! Three years later I was discharged and the first thing I did, even before going home, was fly down to Avon Park, Florida, where my grandfather was waiting for the end in the sun. It was sad as hell. He just sat there on the porch hardly saying anything. He couldn't fish any more because his knees were so swollen from arthritis he could barely walk. A few days later I left for the Bronx. He died before the month was out.

w: Yes, but fishing wasn't over for you. What about the 460-pound broadbill swordfish you caught off Montauk Point in '64; and the six-pound, eleven-ounce brook trout in Labrador in '66; and the ten-pound bonefish in the Bahamas in '70? Weren't those high points? Don't they matter? So Grandpa is dead, and Pop is too old to fish any more. Certainly, that's not the end of everything. Or is it?!

s: You know something? You're a first-class boob. You're the writer, but you don't really know what it's all about. You're too much in love with words to see anything clearly or honestly. Remember Ray Church?

W: Ray who? Hey! It *is* a cabin! See the smoke curling from the chimney? I'll bet Rikhoff and Peper are in there waiting for us by the fire. Mmmm, I can smell the brandy vapors rising from the snifter right now. Keep talking.

S: Try and stop me! Ray Church was a guy my father and I met one day up on the Beaverkill back around '60. He was a hell of a guy who went out of his way to show us some of the better fishing holes, and to introduce us to the farmers whose land we had to cross to fish those holes. All the time I could see that Ray was in great pain, although he tried to hide it. Back at the Antrim Lodge that night, I asked Doug Bury about Ray, and he told us that Ray was a terminal case. Ray Church was *dying,* and he had come up to the Beaverkill so that he could spend his last days on the banks of a river that meant more to him than anything else. Anything! Do you understand that, Writer?!

W: Look! Through the window there! There're Rikhoff and Peper, sipping brandy. Wait! Here! Dry your eyes with this before we go in.

S: Yeah, sure. Anything you say.

# Calm Morning at Landslide

RODERICK HAIG-BROWN



There is a pool on a salmon river in northern Iceland called Holakvorn, or Landslide. The pool is well named. Some long while ago a great slide of rock and earth and gravel came down from the stern face of the mountains on the east bank and swept across the valley floor.

The slide dammed the valley and formed a small shallow lake over its low-lying meadow lands. The lake is still there, a resting place for thousands of geese in the fall and frequented all summer by non-breeding whooper swans which clamber awkwardly out to feed on the meadow grasses. At the lake outlet the river is fully two hundred yards wide, flowing smoothly and evenly, gradually shallowing, spreading more widely yet, until it is riffling over the ford, nowhere deeper than a few inches.

Landslide Pool lies close under the left bank immediately below the lake outlet, shadowed by a little rounded hillock. It is small, no more than six feet deep, fifty or sixty feet wide and perhaps two hundred feet long to where the water breaks out over the rocks at the tail. During the season there are always fish in it, and nearly always fish are moving up to it from the big pool at the head of tidewater half a mile below. It is an exciting pool to fish because one can always see fish moving there, rolling or breaking or occasionally jumping right out, and they take well when there is a wind to ripple the surface of the water, especially if the day is cloudy. Under a bright sun, with the water dead still except for the silky draw of the current, it is said to be almost impossible to catch a fish. That, of course, is just the sort of thing to get a fly fisherman really interested.

Northern Iceland being what and where it is, dead calm days with bright sun are rare enough on Landslide, but I had fished the pool often enough to become familiar with most of its peculiarities before that ideally hopeless time arrived. The first morning I fished it, in 1968, was a day of coldly vicious northwind. I was fishing a fly half a dozen sizes too large—a No. 1 as I recall it—and though several fish rolled at it, I did not have a solid take until I was almost at the tail of the pool. The strike was from a good fish, twelve or fourteen pounds, and it ran at once for the tail, then came back and shattered the pool with an enormous leap right in the center. A moment later the hook came away. After that, though fish after fish followed the big fly, and a few swirled at it, I did not get another solid take and all too soon the morning was over, and I had to move to another beat.

I was fishing a sinking-tip line on that occasion and, not knowing the river, hadn't the wits to change to a smaller fly because the fish kept moving to the one I had; perhaps in that bitter wind it might not have made much difference, although I am pretty sure it would have. Since that day I have rarely fished anything larger than a No. 6 anywhere on the river and have taken most of my fish on 8's and 10's.

There were other days at Landslide, in various states of wind and calm, cloud and sunshine, but even the calm days were not dead still, and one could always wait for a ripple to come on the water. I learned that the fish took best at the end of a long downstream cast on the far side of the pool; there is a sort of ledge there where they lie, shallower than the main body of the pool, and when they are really on they will take the fly firmly within the first foot or two of its swim. They are sometimes easy to catch right down at the tail of the pool, nearly always difficult to persuade right up at the head of the pool.

I was there with two friends one afternoon of intermittent calm. We took it in turns to fish through the pool and managed to hook two or three fish between us, but it was very slow. By crawling to the top of the hillock and peering over, we could see at least twenty fish lying there, shifting a little, sometimes rolling, sometimes turning to flash their sides—good ocean-fresh Atlantic salmon of ten to fifteen pounds. Normally one tries not to walk along the edge of Landslide while there is still any hope of getting a fish from it, but I asked permission to work it upstream with a floating fly and my friends agreed that the time had come for something of the sort.

I circled the hillock and started cautiously, keeping well down. The light was good, and I could see most of the fish clearly, even from down by the water's edge. Several moved as my fly came over them, lifting a little in the water, sometimes turning back in a nervous circle as it drifted past. That is usually a good sign, and I confidently expected a rise with every cast. One ten-pounder almost did the right thing; as the fly came to him he rose up smoothly and gracefully to within an inch or two of the surface, drifted slowly downstream with his nose almost against the fly for six or eight feet, then turned away and down. He would not move again.

All these memories and ideas were with me when I came to the pool one July day in 1971, and there were other ideas too, because I had thought a good deal in the meantime about Landslide and its problems. I believed, as one always does, that I had some answers. At nine-thirty in the morning, the start of legal fishing time, the sun was already high, and everything was dead calm; the lake was flat and motionless; the river from bank to bank reflected the dark mountains, the sky and a few high clouds. A fish broke the still surface out in Bjarnastadir Hylar,

Landslide's lesser brother, a narrow pool about two-thirds of the way straight across the river. I was alone, and it was the time I had been looking for, though my host had said: "Don't bother till the breeze comes up. It probably won't be long." He meant: Don't mess the pool up while it's calm.

I was determined to be deliberate, determined not to mess up the pool, and I hoped that the breeze wouldn't come. I had a four-ounce Winston cane rod, just over eight feet long, with a forward taper floating line (next time it will be double taper). My fly would be a No. 10 Blue Charm, which I knew was as right as it could be. My leader, and the source of a good deal of my faith, was fifteen feet long, tapered to 2X. I wanted the small fly to lay out well at full leader length. I am somewhat lazy about tackle details, so the leader was simply attached to the line with a standard figure of eight instead of a nail knot. It did occur to me to wonder just how I would land or tail a fish with an eight-foot rod and a fifteen-foot leader that could not be safely passed through the top guide, but I felt pretty sure something would work out when the time came.

The head of Landslide Pool is marked by a big rock on the bank, just at the edge of the water. You can and do catch fish above there, but these are essentially travelers, moving on up into the lake. Few fish hold where the water deepens above the rock, and the current there is barely perceptible. So I started in well upstream, throwing a fairly short line and working the fly gently across, moving down a cautious step or two with each cast.

An occasional fish was showing over the ledge on the far side of the pool, and that was where I wanted my fly to be. To get it there I had to be down at least as far as the rock and by that time either crouching or kneeling. But I didn't want to spook any fish from the head of the pool, so my real hope, almost my only hope, was that there would be none there.

Another cast, then another and my fly swung across on a line with the rock. The tackle was working perfectly, the fly looping over at the full extent of the leader, sinking instantly and swimming across very slowly, barely under the surface. One more cast, and a fish showed behind the fly, seeming to surge up at it from downstream but without touching it. A flight of nine swans passed out from the lake, calling occasionally, huge and beautiful in the sunlight. At any other time they would have made the day for me, but now they made me nervous, attacking my fragile concentration.

The fish was lying a little way down from the head of the pool, I decided, and I wanted the fly closer to him. I moved on and cast again, fished it out and cast again. By now I was only twenty feet above the rock and looking into the head of the pool through the smooth surface of the water. Then I saw them, a grilse and two full-sized salmon, looking straight at me, lying calmly abreast of the rock while my heavy fly line swung over them, the fly at the end of its leader now thirty feet downstream. The grilse was a little upstream and a little higher in the water than the other two, a fish of about five pounds, less than half the size of his companions.

I froze, watching them and letting my line straighten out downstream and along the shore. The grilse especially was looking squarely at me, and I felt as embarrassed as a kid caught stealing apples. Very slowly, I backed away upstream. All three kept their watch on my imperceptible going, but they did not move, and in time I could no longer see them. I gave them a still longer time not to see me and backed almost to where I had started in before I recovered my trailing line.

I was certain the grilse was the fish that had showed behind the fly and would have liked to rest the pool and give him a chance to move out of the way—either back into the pool or on up into the lake. But I was afraid the breeze would come up and spoil my project, so I began to fish on down again.

A grilse wouldn't prove much, but there was a chance one of the other fish would get to the fly ahead of him. It seemed unlikely. The fly swam slowly across just above the rock and then, because I was looking for them this time, I could see the fish again. I cast again, the grilse came up to the fly, took it and turned down with it. I tightened against the belly of the line and set the hook. The grilse jumped as he felt it, and I saw the delayed swirls from the tails of the two other fish as they turned away. The ripples from the jump spread across the glossy surface of the pool, and there were more uneasy swirls from fish over the ledge. But I had slacked on the grilse, and he was quiet. I tightened again, very gently, held the line firm and began to back slowly upstream. I spoke unkind words, but softly, to the grilse: "You precocious, interfering runt," I told him. "I'm not going to let you spoil my pool. Why couldn't you stay in the sea another year and keep out of my way? You want to go upstream anyway, so why not now? Come on." And he did come, leading quietly and easily until I had him a couple of hundred feet upstream of the rock.

I started to shorten line then, and he didn't like the feel of it so he ran, not downstream but straight out. He was fast, and he jumped a lot, altogether a good little fish. But he tired after a while and gave me some fumbling practice with the short rod and the long leader. I couldn't reach him with the net. I couldn't get in position to tail him. The beach was somewhat steeper than I liked, but I found the best place, backed far up into the grass, led him on to the gravel, then moved quietly down and picked him up.

I felt quite proud of him. After all, it was dead calm, the sun was high and bright, and he had taken my fly firmly and well. But I wanted a full-grown salmon before the breeze came up, and I had used an hour of calm already.

It was time to abandon some of the care. I went down almost to the rock, swept two or three short casts across, then began to reach out. The two fish were back near the head of the pool, but a little farther downstream and deeper in the water. They seemed unconcerned by my nearness. My next cast was still well short of the shelf, where several good fish were showing. As I worked the fly across the pool a wake followed it, and a fish pulled so lightly that I barely felt him.

The current was faster now and the fly more lively. My next cast was well over the ledge, and again a fish followed. He swirled violently and broke water halfway across the pool. He had pulled hard at the fly, but there was another angry swirl and he was gone. A fish surged at the next cast while the fly was still over the ledge, but I did not feel him. I moved back a step, changed the angle of the next cast slightly upstream and shot two more coils of line. Before I had even begun to fish the fly I was solidly into a good fish.

He ran at once for the tail and jumped there with an enormous crash that sent fish swirling all over the pool. One fish ran straight up the middle of the pool and jumped in sympathy, but my fish was quiet except for a few jarring head-shakes. I walked him up gently, as I had the grilse, hoping I could keep him from exploding again. By the time he was opposite the rock I had recovered a good deal of line, handlining six or eight feet at a time, then working it gently on the reel to dampen the vibrations of the ratchet as much as possible.

He came on past the rock but didn't care much for it. I gave a little line from my hand to two powerful head-shakes, checked it, then saw his body bulge the surface of the water. He was no longer coming upstream, but across. The next thing I knew he was streaking back down the pool again. He broke his run with a heavy surface lunge in the middle of the pool but kept on going and ended it with a slap of his tail just above the rocks where the water breaks over into the rapids. Fortunately he didn't care for the shallow water and came back into the pool.

From then on it was all simple enough except that I had to warn myself again and again as he came near my beaching place: "Don't hurry it, don't hurry it. Wear him right out." So I did, and that was almost a mistake because when I led him in he hadn't the strength to give the flip or two that would push him up the beach. I put the rod down in the grass, walked quietly down and picked him up in both hands. I still wonder what might have happened if he had recovered and swum off before I got there.

The water was still smooth, reflecting sky and mountains in many colors as I retied my fly. I wondered if the pool had been ruined by my violent fish, or if I could go back and take another one just to prove the point more firmly. I decided I didn't really care and lay back in the grass to watch another flight of swans go straggling by; they were calling intermittently and so close that I could see the yellow on their beaks. I felt the breeze come then and saw a few cat's paws streaking the lake's surface. They reached the river and ruffled it. Then the breeze was steady and freshening.

I changed to a nine-foot leader, tied the same fly back on and went straight to the rock at the head of the pool. My third cast hooked another fish. He ran me out of the pool and almost down to the ford before I could get him under control and tail him.

*Nick did not like to fish with other men of the river. Unless they were of your party, they spoiled it.*

ERNEST HEMINGWAY, *Big Two-Hearted River*

# The Challenge and the Prize

LAMAR UNDERWOOD



Where would guys like Nick Adams fish now?

The man who lived in Papa Hemingway's classic short story which relates the pleasures of fishing and camping on an isolated trout stream would find his rigid philosophy unworkable in most of America, where the sprawling megalopolises have shouldered against, bruised and ruined the most convenient trout rivers.

The plunderers and the crowds, the bureaucrats and the

politicos had already begun to spoil the easy-to-reach trout water in Nick's time. That's why he took a train deep into the pine forests of upper Michigan and walked for miles to find his good place on the Big Two-Hearted. Nick knew that to get to the best water to fish and to camp a man had to leave the highways, shoulder a pack, and use his legs and sweat a little.

Two of us who could never turn off our dreams of the Nick Adams type of experience had come to a place where a river of cold sweet water ran dark and rock-slashed through a canyon of spruce, then curved sun-dappled and chuckling through a low plain of alders. At the beginning of the alder lowlands just where the river boiled from the darker forest, a pine-covered hillock loomed beside the water. A tent was pitched there, and a few yards away a thin veil of smoke rose against a horizon that was splashed with pure gold. Overhead a pair of nighthawks zoomed and climbed, and ducks passed on whispering wings. A loon called forlornly from some distance. Surrounded by a clutter of packs and rods and gear, we sat on a log beside the fire and sipped whiskey from plastic cups. Occasionally, we looked down the slope toward the river where a canoe had been pulled up on the bank and turned over. Still wet and dripping across the broad bottom of the craft were a pair of dressed brook trout.

For Jim and me—weaned on crowded campgrounds and hatchery trout, but touched by the deep effect of an unforgettable piece of angling literature—the dream of true wilderness fishing had changed to delicious reality during a fantastic experience when a river we thought had betrayed us finally yielded a treasure more enduring than a mere good catch of fish.

The Drowning River pours out of the spruce flatlands northeast of Lake Nipigon, in Ontario, and winds across solid wilderness to spill eventually into the trout-famed Albany River. Only at its source, near the railroading village of Nakina, is the Drowning close to any sort of human enterprise. From there it quickly breaks free to flow unmolested except for the occasional probes of trappers and adventuresome anglers.

I first saw the river glistening far below the wing as Len McMillen banked the Norseman into his final approach. The next eight days would either prove or deflate the real kicker behind the outfitter's description of the river. "You will catch the specks," he said. "They are there—big and plenty."

As the floatplane dropped closer to the thick carpet of trees, the green expanse parted, and a narrow lake simmered in the sun. McMillen eased back on the throttle and set us down softly.

Jim and I piled our packs on the campsite while Mac unstrapped the canoe from the pontoon and tied it in the shallows. "See you a week from tomorrow at Supawn Lake," he called as he jumped back aboard the plane. A moment later he was roaring over the trees out of sight. I dug out our map and looked around. Relief Lake stretched calm and bright toward a distant line of trees. I located our position on the map and found the outlet—where the Drowning once again became a living river and continued its run. The map showed that some seventy twisting miles downstream, past numerous wavy-lined markings with scary notations like R15′, R32′, the river came within two miles of our pickup point, Supawn Lake. Once we left Relief Lake, we would be committed to whatever horrors or delights the Drowning had in store for us.

"Well, we're committed," Jim said. "If we bust our ass, help'll be a long time getting to us."

"Let's get busy."

The mid-July day was unseasonably warm for that area, but the sweat and work of setting up camp seemed to be cleaning the urban-life rust from my psyche. We cooled off with a dip in the lake. Later that evening we probed the lake with wobbling spoons and jigs, but the pike and walleyes we expected to swarm over our lures never materialized. The first slivers of worry crept into my mind.

"Too warm for this lake stuff maybe," Jim said. "Seems odd to think that this far north you have to worry about heat puttin' 'em off, but I guess it happens."

Back in camp, we enjoyed the first drink of the trip to the serenade of loons and the sizzle of steaks while the dying sun burned on the top of the trees. The air had some crispness now, and a little breeze had come up to dispel most of the mosquitoes that had had us reaching for the repellent while we pitched camp that afternoon.

That night I lay in my sleeping bag and tried to envision the spot where the Drowning tore free of the lake and once again became a roaring river. The honest fact was that although Jim and I thought we could handle the river, we were not what you'd call expert canoeists. We were relying on our basic knowledge and good judgment to get us through most spots and figured to take on the really dangerous water by roping down or portaging. Now that I could practically feel the terror of the current, I wondered if we had bitten off too large a chunk of action. This was close to the edge of the notorious hinterland area that Ontario had at one time closed to fishermen as a result of repeated disasters. These rough rivers and sprawling spruce forests are no place for weakness or mistakes.

The morning broke gray and still with air like a warm, moist blanket. As we prepared breakfast the mosquitoes, unhampered now by wind, bored in with relentless assaults. We had expected bugs and had plenty of repellent on hand, but now I was questioning the wisdom of our having disdained mosquito nets for our heads. Paddling down the open lake, we temporarily forgot the presence of the pests and enjoyed the feel of the canoe wedging through the quiet water. The lake ended in a long cove that narrowed between walls of willow and spruce. The rumble of the rapids rose ominously, and mild current began to tug at the canoe. Swifter then, the water swung around a gentle bend and spilled from the lake in an explosion of foam and spray. We dug hard for the left bank where a semblance of a portage trail led through the trees.

Immediately, the mosquitoes were on us in clouds. We grabbed the repellent and slathered ourselves with it. My experiences in southern Ontario's provincial parks, where portage trails are maintained like paths, had not prepared me for the task of getting our canoe and equipment across that brushy, log-choked trace. When the last load had finally been dropped on the far side, we slumped wearily—but not for long. The mosquitoes were taking advantage of our sweat-diluted, fading repellent. We quickly reloaded the canoe, taking particular care to get the weight forward, and shot out into the current.

There was no time to relax. We were being sucked toward a long stretch where boulders were ripping the current into white streaks. The bank seemed to be flying past. Then we were there, cutting in and out between the leering rocks, skimming across the tops of jagged edges that loomed just beneath the surface. In the bow, Jim was making lightning decisions on our course, and I keyed my strokes from his actions—a long sweep here, a pull-over there, braking for a moment, praying all the time. Finally the current slacked off.

Jim let the paddle rest on his lap for a moment. "It'd be fun, if it just wasn't so damn serious. I'm scared, man."

"You can't run and you can't hide," I added. "Anyway, the mosquitoes are gone."

The mention of the pests reminded me to splash on more repellent. Jim had a can up front, but I started looking for the small pack that held a few miscellaneous items and our full stock of repellent. I couldn't find it. Jim joined the search. Finally we beached the canoe and started moving gear, searching frantically. The pack was gone—left on the portage trail.

There was no need for a staff conference on the seriousness of the situation. With no mosquito nets and now no repellent, we were going to take a beating. A mosquito bit me on the neck, and I slapped him sharply. How many stings will it take, I wondered, before the swarms reduce us to blubbering idiots?

We were free of the pests as long as we stayed in the current. We began to enjoy the stream and the country and the feel of the canoe as it responded to our strokes when some stretch of rocky water threatened.

We pitched camp that afternoon on a parklike pine-covered ridge where the breeze sang in the trees and gave us relief from the mosquitoes.

The spot was so pleasant that we were tempted to spend a couple of days there. However, our casts into the rapids and pools failed to turn up a single trout, and we decided to push on the next morning.

That was a day of terror and hardship. During hours of light rain, we rode the belly of the black water through the heavy spruce forests. Rapids appeared every few miles, some so fierce that we were forced to rope the canoe through. Staggering over the jagged, slippery boulders along the edge of the stream, we were literally covered with mosquitoes and waged a desperate struggle to keep a grip on ourselves. We had donned our jackets, covered our hands with socks and tied sweaters around our heads—still the pests attacked. We reached a portage, but fishing was out of the question. The trail led through a low swamp, and by the time we got the canoe and gear across we were practically feverish.

We dug out the tent and began rigging it up. Finally we zipped the fly shut and collapsed inside. For a long time we were oblivious to the mosquitoes that had swarmed in with us. Eventually we got to work putting them out of business while sheer clouds of their brothers hovered outside the door and rear window. A bottle of aspirin was the only medicine we had because our first aid supplies had been in the accessory pack with the repellent. My skin felt as though it were on fire with welts. It was some time before we felt like talking.

"We're in a real jam," Jim said. "We can stay here and wait to be taken out like a couple of whipped dogs, or we can try and go on—maybe get into even worse trouble."

"A couple of times today, I thought we had really bought it," I said. "We missed some rocks by inches that could've ripped the bottom out of that canoe. And once we almost got sideways."

"I can't see enough up there in the bow," Jim said. "The bugs are swarming in my eyes, mouth, everywhere."

"Let's go on, though. Long as we can. Maybe we'll get some wind, or get out of this tight, forest stretch."

We ate little that night and slept fitfully. In the morning, the air was still dank and heavy. We moved like condemned men as we climbed out of our sleeping bags and got ready. As we pulled down the tent, the mosquitoes were on us in clouds that made me fight to keep from saying, "The hell with it!" Finally we loaded and shoved off, and for a while it felt good to feel the pull of the current and be on the move again.

The rapids came more frequently now. We would ride some smooth, dark stretch for a while, then hear the first hint of white-water roar—subtle at first as we stroked on wearily, hoping the sound was some trick of the wind, then unmistakable and depressing as we drew nearer. More than anything, we wanted to stay on the water, to get on down this bad-luck river as fast as possible. Somehow, despite our feverish condition, we summoned up the courage to yield to the toughest stretches and rope down along the shore. Stumbling down through the shallows and along the log-choked portage trails while the mosquitoes swarmed in clouds, we came to the limits of our endurance.

We lay in the tent for what seemed like hours. Finally Jim said, "We've got to get a break or give up. We just can't take much more of this."

We huddled over the map. About three hours downstream was a spot that the outfitter had touted as having the grandest scenery of the trip. "There's nothing beautiful about these dark spruce forests," I said. "Maybe that's open country."

I don't know how we managed to get moving the next morning, but we did. Not long afterward, a slight breeze began

to blow upriver, and the mosquitoes gradually disappeared. What a relief it was to shed the bundles of clothing that we had to wear to stop the bites. Soon the rain stopped and cracks of light began to show in the grayness overhead. The country began to change character. The trees were shorter, and brushy flats stretched away between the clusters of timber. Then the sun burst through, and the sunshine and open country were like another world compared with the dark tunnels we had been running.

Suddenly Jim pointed to the bank ahead of the canoe. "Look at those trout!" he said.

At the entrance to a little cove where a small creek spilled into the Drowning, the slashing rises of brook trout could be seen. At the same moment I saw the fish, something else grabbed my attention. The distant rumble of rapids could be heard. We drifted quietly for a moment, watching the trout and listening carefully. It was unmistakable now. Those rapids were at the spot we had been trying to reach.

We spurted on downstream. A couple of bends below the spring hole, the treeline ended abruptly. Alder flats stretched away on each side. The world was sunny, breezy and practically free of mosquitoes. Just before the point where the water spilled over a low falls and through a small stretch of rapids, a hillock loomed above the tops of the alders. We tied the canoe and walked up the grassy bank.

A pair of big pines stood beside a lawnlike clearing that overlooked the river and the alder plain. Suddenly, I was no longer aware that I was sick with mosquito bites or that I ached anywhere at all. We had found our Shangri-La. So swiftly had we dropped downriver that we would be able to spend the rest of the trip at this spot and make the run downriver to our rendezvous lake in one day. I looked at Jim. He was miserably wet and fatigued, but he was smiling.

We spent the remainder of the day resting and setting up the camp. Every chore was carried out with a sharp sense of pleasure and anticipation. Dry clothes, warm food and a good nap made us feel a lot better. By the time the long Ontario afternoon was edging into twilight, we felt like fishing.

Jim took the paddle and eased the canoe toward the creek opening. My tiny spinner flashed in the fading sunlight, then sailed into the shadows along the shore. Too far out, I thought. Jim was holding the canoe in perfect position. I reeled hurriedly for another cast; then I felt the sudden weight of some furious live thing smash into the lure and try to carry it away. The rod danced, alive, arching strongly. My wrist firmed against the joyous pressure that shot up the rod, through my hand, up my arm, and into my soul. I laughed aloud. Swirls of vague form and quick colors broke the dark surface. The monofilament sang as it sawed in easy circles. It cut toward the canoe, the rod tip bowing to the water alongside. Jim had the net down beside the water. The swirls were getting close when Jim's hand suddenly reached down.

There was the trip's first trout: sagging and dripping, clean and longlined, colored like all the greatest dawns and sunsets you've ever seen. He was 3½ pounds of fish that had never seen a hatchery. I kept hefting and admiring him. You'd think I hadn't scored in years. And I hadn't—not like this—ever.

It was Jim's turn now. We slid alongside a rock, changed places and eased back to the hot spot. Jim's spoon plunked into the pool. Something swirled a few feet in toward shore. "Got him!" Jim exclaimed, and I looked up to see the kind of picture that burns into memory: the dying sun showing through the dark line of trees upriver; Jim outlined against the glow, his arms high, his rod curved in a straining and trembling bow. The fish swirled and dived and worked heavily against the whip of the rod. Gradually, Jim gained line. Some deep runs directly beneath the canoe decided the issue. The mouth of the net swept under the tired fish, another three-pounder.

During the next few days we came to call that spring-creek area our "honey hole." We caught and released trout after trout along that stretch. The weather held bright and breezy, and every day was a pleasure from the first scent of coffee in the morning until we dropped off to the sound of the rapids at night.

Finally, time had run out. Coming back to camp in the evening, the canoe scraped against the sand bottom on the bank for the last time. We climbed out stiffly, and Jim put a match to the kindling and firewood that we always left ready for the evening. I looked downstream beyond the falls toward the rapids. "Be right back," I said.

There was still enough light to see the boulders as I scrambled along the edge of the stream to get opposite the place where the water swept past the last white-tailed bulges of rock before curving away smooth and black. Fishing this pool had become an evening ritual, but not one trout had taken my flies or spinners. Jim figured the area to be too far downstream from the spring-fed stretch we had discovered. But somehow the way in which this pool tailed off into that heavy flow spelled big trout to me.

Normally I had fished this stretch with the same tackle I used upriver: a floating line for flies or with small spinners. I wanted this last shot to be a good one and had put on a heavy, fast-sinking line and big Mickey Finn streamer.

I placed the cast farther upstream than usual. The line curved across the dark ribbon of current and straightened into the deeper shadows along the tree-covered bank. I could feel the line working deeper and deeper as it swung downstream with the current. Finally, it was well downstream, and I stripped in a few inches, then a few more. Still nothing happened.

Next, I began stripping in a foot at a time, and suddenly a

fish hit and was going away in a solid, weighty pull. I let the reel scream and wondered if Jim could hear it. Then I panicked and braked the spool hard. Too hard, I realized in one agonizing second as the line tightened hard against the weight. Then came that gut-aching feeling of slackness, and I reeled in slowly, the reel click shattering the stillness.

So he was gone, the best fish of the trip, maybe even the last big, wild trout I'll ever hook. I wondered how many times I would get back to these wild, free places where these fish live? Maybe never again.

I put down my disappointment as I walked toward the camp. Why never? I said to myself. Hell No! Never! I'll walk, climb or paddle to wherever I have to go, or fish the difficult pools, or in tangles, or the places everybody overlooks. Pay what it costs. Do what it takes. That style worked here on the Drowning. It'll work for me again.

I had come into the big glow of the campfire. Jim handed me my drink without saying a thing about the damn-fool way I was grinning.

# Monique and the Stupid Salmon

CHARLES RITZ



Monique is a little blue-eyed girl, slightly built but very athletic; a girl with a great temperament and a zest for verbal battles and discussions. Her one regret is that she did not study Law. She is also a fine wing shot, but at the time of which I write all she knew about fishing had been gained from watching the *pêcheurs au coup*—the British term them coarse anglers—drifting red worms or maggots along the bed of the Seine, below the Eiffel Tower. She always referred to my own efforts as "fly swatting."

For years I hoped, some day, to introduce Monique to *Salmo salar.* But in her view fly-fishing lacked action: it was a pastime for those incapable of more active pursuits. So it was that I gave up all thought of taking her to Norway *unless* I could find an aquarium pool—a tidal pool at the foot of a waterfall, as close as possible to the sea and stocked with fresh-run salmon ready to take a fly the moment it hit the water.

In the spring of 1967, at the Normandy Hotel in Deauville (the Touque flows nearby, a stream with sea trout to fifteen pounds in its lower reaches) we met Albert and his charming wife, Miette. Here was my man. He had fished most of Norway's finest rivers and employed a bevy of lawyers whose job it was to contact the Norwegian peasants who owned the fishing rights on streams flowing through their farms.

In July of that year Albert leased two rivers, about a hundred miles from the famous Laerdal, and offered me a rod. His description of one part of the water matched the pool I dreamed of finding.

"One river," he said, "has a pool at the foot of the first waterfall, only a mile from the fjord. It's full of salmon and sea trout. The pool is tidal, of course, rising and falling twice every twenty-four hours. You can fish it at an ideal level for the fly four times a day—twice on the flood tide, twice on the ebb—and the fish are always active at those times. Fishing between ten A.M. and six P.M., and without fishing hard, Miette and I usually take half a dozen from that spot. They're not big fish, but being fresh-run they are great fighters. And, Charles, you must bring Monique."

This was my chance. Had I known the outcome I would have declined there and then, but not being clairvoyant I got no further than the thought that all fishermen exaggerate. (When sport is poor they explain it all quite happily by reasoning that the fish have not yet arrived or the water is colored; it is too high or too low; the sun is too bright or a storm has been threatening for days. Alternatively, fish are scarce and few have been taken anywhere.) But this time, Albert had to be right. There would be no second chance with Monique.

I accepted his invitation and faced the next hurdle. How could I persuade Monique to come with me? In the end we compromised: she promised to stay for three days and I guaranteed her at least two salmon.

There was one other problem. Monique had never cast with a salmon rod in her life and it was essential that she should learn to cast correctly before starting to fish. Thank Heaven, the pond of Le Tir aux Pigeons in the Bois de Boulogne was only a ten-minute ride from the Ritz. Pierre and I battled through six hours of practice, teaching her to throw a high back line until she became casting-conscious. Throughout that time I feared that Monique would quit at any moment.

Had I but known it—and all that was to transpire before this saga could end—I should have realized that this might well have been the best thing that could happen.

When we arrived at the Sunnfjord Hotel in Forde I started to unpack our luggage, only to find that the bag containing our fishing clothes—boots, waders, raincoats, etc.—was missing.

Monique was hopping mad. She hates rain, cold weather and discomfort in any form.

"Charles," she said, in a manner that left me in no doubt that she was in earnest, "this is ridiculous. I have no intention of fishing barefoot, the water here is too cold. Haven't I always told you to count the bags before you leave the airport? When is the next plane to Paris?"

In those few moments all my planning and conniving counted for nothing. I told her that there was no plane for two days, but that I would reserve a seat for her, immediately. And I did. I also cabled the Ritz, asking them to ship the missing bag with all speed. Monique could blame the airline, but I knew where it was: at the Ritz, Paris.

Luckily, Monique was allowed to spin from the bank, but the jinx that had traveled with us still exerted its baleful influence: the spinning reel developed clutch trouble. Monique was suddenly fast to a nice grilse—the first salmon she had ever contacted—but though she reeled in and in, the fish remained stationary.

It was a moment I shall long remember. Monique yelling that she had a big fish, a very big fish; reeling like mad and cursing the salmon because it moved not one inch toward her; ordering Ehrling, our ghillie, to wade into midstream and net her catch, without realizing that he, poor man, only wore hip boots and that the water out there was exceptionally deep.

Thinking to ease the situation, I took hold of the line and handed it to her with the instruction that she should drop the rod, hold the line tight and walk up the bank. This simple and very practical maneuver met with unexpected opposition.

"I did not come here," she said, and those blue eyes were positively icy, "to handline fish like the mackerel catchers at Deauville."

Somehow, that grilse was drawn into the shallows. Ehrling netted it, the sun shone and Monique was as happy as a small boy with his first gudgeon.

"Charles . . . cancel my plane."

I dared not look too happy. Casually, I told her that the missing bag would arrive next morning.

"Fine!" she exclaimed. "I don't like this spoon fishing. Tomorrow we shall have waders and I can fish with the fly. I'll show you how to catch salmon."

The following day the river was clear, but still a little too high. In order to make casting easier for her, I suggested that she should fish from the high rock beside the waterfall, a point from which even a badly cast line would soon straighten in the fast current.

"Nothing doing!" said Monique. "You don't think I'm crazy enough to risk my life for one of these fish?"

I replied that I had a very strong rope and she would be perfectly safe. "Darling love, just tie the rope round your waist and I will stand behind you, holding it tight. My felt soles cannot possibly slip on the rock."

During the discussion which followed, the rope, my felt shoes and my own ability to save her from a dreadful fate were all questioned and somehow survived. She finally agreed. But first, she said, we would try it without the encumbrance of rod and line. White with fear and convinced that she was risking her life, Monique edged forward on the big rock. And at that moment my luck changed: a salmon leapt into the air from the very heart of the water I wanted her to fish.

I do believe that her fears had vanished before the fish hit the surface. "My God!" she exclaimed, "did you see that fish jump? Quick, Charles, the rod. I must get him. And, please, lengthen this confounded rope."

Her first cast was too short, too close to the rock.

"Monique, more line, please."

Then the back-cast missed me by inches. I sat down, fast.

"Still more line, Monique. That's better: now let the line swing towards the rock."

The tubefly hit the water in midstream and started to swing out of the main current.

"Charles! The line is pulling hard, very hard. I must have a fish. Oh, please, help me!"

There was a fifty yard run, a flash of silver as the fish jumped, then a slack line and goodbye salmon. No cussing, no orders; just a poor little lady in tears.

For the next two days the salmon showed no interest in the fly. I asked Monique to concentrate on improving her casting and to master the high back line. She agreed and after an hour's practice she stopped looking forward and watching the line whip the water. Instead, she followed my advice and looked at the tip of her rod when it reached twelve o'clock. She noticed that the rod continued to move until it dropped to three o'clock. I helped her, holding the rod with her as she cast.

"Watch the rod, nothing else, and don't worry about how the line falls on the water. Try to stop the rod before it reaches one o'clock—that's absolutely vital."

I took my hand from the rod and to my great satisfaction both the rod tip and the line stayed up.

"Well done," I told her. "Now, please try another twenty casts, and look up every time."

Her technique was excellent. When I allowed her to look forward again Monique was casting a superbly straight line and her immediate comment reflected the boundless enthusiasm so typical of her.

"Charles, I have it. Oh, how wonderful. Look . . . I can cast exactly as you wanted me to."

A fish broke water and she was fast to a small salmon.

"What shall I do?" she called. "He's pulling so hard, I can't hold him."

I told her to press with the index finger of her left hand against the inside face of the reel. Not too much pressure. Let the fish run whenever it seems to pull too hard. And when it stops, pump it toward the bank by lifting and lowering the rod, winding line onto the reel as the rod goes down.

Fortunately, the fish soon weakened and Monique, bubbling with energy, was once more in command.

"Ehrling, get the net. Hurry now: if I lose this fish I shall hate you."

Ehrling had no intention of being hated by anyone. A few minutes later the fish was on the bank and Monique stood there admiring the first silver king she had ever caught with a fly.

This, she said, was the greatest moment in her life. She was so happy, so thrilled. But why had the fish stopped fighting so soon?

"I want another one. Perhaps I should change the fly?"

I persuaded her to leave the fly where it was and move with me to what I knew to be the best part of the pool—a small hole or pocket in the center of the main current, not deep but a fine resting place for salmon and one used by all the fish going upstream towards the big waterfall. In fact, that fall is too high for them. After many unsuccessful attempts to negotiate it, the fish drop back and eventually find the smaller waterfall behind the island, a natural fish ladder.

The hole we made for has a nice swirl of water and when the current is not too fast it is possible to sink a tubefly vertically below the surface. There it remains stationary or moving gently with the water for a full second before the line pulls it away. In brief, ideal conditions in which to induce My Lord Salmon to take a fly without having to rush after it.

I confess that I was anxious that Monique should catch another fish or two. Other considerations apart, it would remove all risk of our speedy return to Paris. I cast twice to find out how quickly the fly would start to drag and had I been lucky I would have handed her the rod.

Those two casts revealed that the position was OK for an experienced fisherman, but not for a tenderfoot, not even for one with a high back-cast. It was a matter of line speed and the fact that the fly must hit the water first. This could only be done with a perfectly executed and very fast, very high forward-cast, raising the rod point at the last moment to speed the fly's penetration of the surface layer.

My suggestion that she should wait until the current slowed a little was greeted with the utmost suspicion and contempt. I had, of course, seen a fish and wanted to take it myself. I was, she said, an old fox, but not cunning enough by half.

The Old Fox, who had seen nothing whatever, invited her to go ahead. Fifteen minutes later, no results. I moved away. Fishing some fifty yards downstream, I caught two salmon.

"Charles . . . let me have your place."

We changed over and I give my word that I fished only the edges of the pool, taking great care not to spoil it for her. Yet I

was lucky enough to land a good fish while Monique's best casting produced nothing at all.

Again came the request to change places, and again I agreed.

It so happens that, when hunting, Monique always shoulders her gun as she walks. She did the same thing with her salmon rod on this occasion, wading slowly upstream with a few yards of line trailing behind her. As I walked down I heard a splash, a fish took her fly and that quiet pool echoed with the song of a reel.

"Ehrling! Ehrling, I have one; get the net. Charles! Help me!"

It was a brute of a fish, a salmon that stopped dead when it reached the slow water opposite the bench where we used to sit and watch when fish were not taking. Minutes later it was on the bank, a fifteen pounder, and Monique was jumping to conclusions that I found quite shattering.

"There it is, Charles; a bigger fish than any of yours. Could you ask for more definite proof that all your talk of tactics is so much nonsense? These salmon are stupid. All you have to do is drop the line in the water and walk upstream."

What could I say? That was exactly what she had done. I knew better, of course, but deep down I began to wonder. And what would I have to endure when fishermen and their wives met at future cocktail parties?

With the passing of time, Monique's account of that day's fishing has become a masterpiece. It includes a reference to the fact that though I said a change of fly was unnecessary she decided otherwise and picked out a pattern she knew the salmon would like—an old Jock Scott I had carelessly left in her fly box. She adds—so help me!—that she is now certain that female salmon prefer pastel shades and male fish the darker hues.

My one consolation is that after ten years I finally succeeded in landing *her,* hook, line and sinker. We were married last summer. I am still wondering who was the most stupid: Monique, me or the salmon!

# A Balm for Fishlessness

ARNOLD GINGRICH



When you're having a blank day in fishing it doesn't mean, of course, that you're doing nothing that day. The chances are you actually work harder, change flies more often, agonize over every aspect of what you're doing to see whether there's anything you shouldn't be doing that you are or that you aren't doing that you should, and as far as you're concerned, the only ones who are doing nothing that day are the fish, because you're doing everything that you can think of.

(Surprisingly often, the one way to snap out of a prolonged spell of fishlessness is to try something—almost anything—that you haven't tried for a long time. If you can find a fly in your box that you haven't used for the last four seasons, that may do it. Sometimes it even works to find a fly of which you can say, in all honesty, that you've never yet caught anything on it. Fish are so perverse that they'll go to almost any lengths to prove you wrong, even in such an extreme instance as that.)



Similarly, when we say that our minds are a total blank, it's almost never true, unless we're asleep, and even then dreams keep the motor idling, so to speak, even if we don't remember the dreams when we wake up. Remembering that this is supposed to be a contemplative pastime, I sometimes try to check up on myself while I'm fishing, to see if I can get any inkling of what I'm contemplating, and I have yet to be successful at it. Sleepless nights, or white nights, as the French call them, are pretty much the same thing. Nights we'd swear we haven't shut an eye, scientists assure us that we have, without realizing it, and they have devised various instruments that will prove it to us if we persist in our doubt. It's just that we think we're not sleeping, as we so often think we're not thinking, when of course we are.

By the same token, solitude is the norm in sport fishing, even for those who are frightened by the very thought of being alone. Most people I know have fishing partners, without whom they wouldn't dream of going off alone on even the briefest of trips. But what they forget, in all the togetherness of meals and lodging and entertainment activities that take place before and after fishing, is how little actual fishing time they actually spend together. Each has his own section of stream to fish, and normally they are either out of each other's sight or at least out of anything less than shouting distance apart. The actual fishing, even for people who wouldn't dream of going to a movie or even a restaurant alone, is a solitary act.

As Uncle Thad Norris best pointed out, better than a lifetime ago, in the chapter devoted to "The Pleasures of Solitary Fly Fishing" in his 1864 volume, *The American Angler's Book,* and as we've all seen in actual practice, fishing is essentially a solo sport. What comes before and after may not be, but the fishing itself is. Yet, although I fish alone much more of the time than when there's anybody else around, and have never felt that fishing had to be shared to be enjoyed, still I must admit that, if there were some practical way to count and measure my thought processes while I fish, it would show that I think much more about other people than I do about myself. And I'm sure I'm not unique, or even unusual, in this respect.

We all tend to do a certain amount of reading about any subject in which we have developed more than a casual interest, and also there's a certain inevitability, if you do anything long enough and often enough, that you're going to meet a number of people who are doing it too. So, unless you're hiding out somewhere as a fugitive from justice or are a downed airman on an atoll, living off a survival kit, you don't have to be either a chronic joiner or a rampant extrovert to find that there's an inescapable element of companionship in your fishing, however solitary you may be in its actual practice.

In a sense, I never fish alone, in that a good share of the time, even before dawn and after dark, I'm apt to be fishing "with" somebody. It may be somebody I've never known nor ever will, or it may be somebody I have known but will never see again. Because it's with somebody who is in any case absent from the actual scene of my fishing, my own more-than-middle age and the law of averages team up to furnish the likelihood that it is somebody who is no longer living. But that's only natural, in any event; you can learn more from the dead than from the living, if only because there are so many more of them. But I still don't mean that all my fishing is "down among the dead men." I'm as ready as the next to take a tip from any passing stranger, when I'm somewhere out on a stream. And a great deal of my fishing is done with people, dead or alive, with whom I have fished in the past and, in the latter instance, will undoubtedly fish with again but are in any case not around right now.

Still, most of these silent conversations I hold with those absentees, dead or alive, whenever I'm fishing alone, have to do with things I've learned from them, whether in conversation or in practice or in print. For instance, there's one sentence of Theodore Gordon's that must cross my mind practically every other time I find myself out fishing. "Cast your fly with confidence" is probably the most valuable single thing Theodore Gordon ever said, if we but have the wit to interpret it in such a way as to benefit from its meaning. There's no question that your expectations of a certain fly are a large part of the reason why it will produce for you (when it does), and the same thing can work in reverse. We all tend, for insufficient reasons, to get too high on some flies and too down on others. I wouldn't give you the time of day for a Muddler Minnow, for instance, but I can remember a time when, stiff with Mucilin, and hence diving and bobbing on the surface in a fast retrieve, a Muddler had the effect of a veritable Pied Piper. It led swarms of rainbows to chase after it, and then one after another of them to pounce on it, like a cat on a ball of yarn, when it moved fast enough that it appeared to be about to get away. But I can also remember one night when Al McClane and I, in a canoe on a lake near the Upper Beaverkill, kept trying for hours to repeat that experience and got an ignominious skunking for our pains. I've since watched other anglers fish a Muddler as if it were a nymph, with the slowest of slow retrieves, and pick off one rainbow after another. But let me just start playing "monkey see, monkey do" on such an occasion, and even once or twice with the very same Muddler, and for me it goes on strike and won't produce a thing no matter how I fish it.

"Moderation in all things," Theodore Gordon probably should have added, though perhaps he assumed we'd have sense enough to take that for granted. For it is one thing to "cast your fly with confidence," which probably helps you to make the cast with greater care and keeps you more alert as you fish it out, for the strike that you so confidently expect, but it is quite another to go on flailing the water with it for hours on end determined to make it work again just because it worked yesterday.

Of the two extremes, it would probably be better to start with the assumption that the very fact that it did work yesterday *reduces* its chances of working today, so it would be better to invest some of that confidence in a fly that you haven't given a fair chance, after this one has shown that it no longer possesses yesterday's magic. About the only certainty in fly fishing is that a fly won't catch fish if it stays in its box. There's no sure way to guarantee its success, but that's the one sure way to implement its failure. Knowing this, I ought to try to pace myself to use some of the flies that I now consistently pass over when I'm reaching for one of my favorites. If I would do this regularly, I feel sure it would reduce the number of my fishless nights. But my big trouble is that I overreact to both success and failure.

Let me catch a four-pounder on no matter what fly and I'm ready to make that fly the foundation of a new religion, and I'm chucking it at every poor fish in sight for the next month, until I make them all so sick of the sight of it as to obviate its last chance of enticing any of them. I've done this with the Montana nymph, the Zug Bug, the little Royal Coachman streamer, and most recently with a New Zealand streamer called the Mrs. Simpson. Whenever this happens to me, and it happens fairly often, I have only one recourse, and that is to get as far away as possible, both from the type and the size of fly, as well as the method of fishing it. In short, to start over—acting as if I hadn't been fishing at all up to this point and choosing a fly as if it were my first choice of the day.

The alternative, I suppose, is to give up fishing entirely, but though a lot of us threaten that with practically chronic frequency, going home in a huff as often as three nights in a row, I can't seem to think of anybody who ever actually carried out that threat. We all seem to be back again the next night, apparently ready to go on fishing, with or without the least sign of encouragement from the fish. The feeling about fishing is a lot like that about sex, that of course it's better when it's good, but it's not bad, even when it isn't. And for some, it must be realized, there's even a lot of fun in thinking about it. This last element must account, in large part, for what keeps us everlastingly at it. The number of fishless days, it seems, can never be great enough to cure us of this addiction.

Of course, the more you fish, the sooner you reach that stage where you'd rather put the fish back for somebody else to catch, or simply to catch them again yourself rather than take them home to eat, or even to have mounted, for the subsequent amazement of all and sundry. Most wives, for one thing, are less than ecstatic over mounted fish as elements of home decoration, and, for another, people who mount fish are nowadays even harder to come by than fish that merit being mounted.

You'd think, then, that as long as we're not going to keep the fish anyway, going fishless wouldn't be such a dire fate as to warrant our being classified as hardship cases. What's so bad about being skunked, if you set out resolved to return as empty-handed as if you had been anyway? And why moan about the one that got away, when you were going to put him back again even if he hadn't? Well, this is where the element of thinking

about it enters in. It only matters, of course, if you think it does. And, boy, you find it very hard to think of anything, at least at that moment, that matters more. In fact, the great thing about fishing is that there are very few activities that are open to all men on a virtually equal basis and that can provide you with occasions to feel quite so deeply, to care quite that much.

It's all very well for Izaak Walton to have settled the question centuries ago, on a purely philosophical basis, by reminding us that no man can be said to have lost that which he never had. On that basis, of course, there is no such thing as a lost fish. But if it doesn't exist, why does it hurt so much?

I've never felt such intense compassion for anyone in my life as I felt for Ernest Hemingway in Bimini in 1936, when a marlin that looked the size of a tank car in the sun got away after some thirty jumps, and the hand-forged hook, looking the size of an anchor, came back pulled out and straightened like a bent bobby-pin. And if I felt that bad, then how bad did he feel?

Nature, in one of her few acts of kindness, is supposed to have made our memories of pain mercifully short. We can remember, as an abstract fact, that this or that experience caused us pain, but it is scientifically posited that our mental mechanism lacks the means of really re-enacting the actual sensation of pain. So, all right, it does stop hurting, but no man who has ever lost a truly noteworthy fish has ever forgotten it either. By the same token, the pain of losing a good fish, after he has taken, and after you've had him on long enough to sample the fight that is in him, is a relative joy, a privilege and an honor, compared to the awful ignominy and the bleak despair of casting hours on end and never once feeling the least tug or pull or slightest twitch, by way of response to your endless flailings.

Skunked indeed! A real live skunk, aside from being very pretty, smells downright sweet, as against the ineffable stench of defeat in the fisherman's nostrils.

For the safeguarding of one's sanity under these circumstances, there are only two things to do. (Oh, I suppose there are three, if your psychic stamina as an angler is so frail that you can consider resorting, at such junctures, to the use of salmon eggs, or live minnows or frogs or worms. So maybe we'd better put it on the basis that there are only two things to do that are thinkable in present company.)

First, you can go on doing what you're doing, trusting to the law of averages that after *x* many thousands of casts you're going to catch *something.* The only way for the sentient angler to do this indefinitely, against the steadily rising counter-pressure of tedium, is by concentrating intently on the exact shape and color and size of fish you have caught in the past, making this very same cast with this very same fly in this very same spot or in a spot very nearly like this. If taking this mental inventory takes you no longer than it would take most of us, then five minutes is about all this exercise is good for. Sometimes, though very rarely, five minutes of this is enough to produce a strike. When it has happened to me, it has restored my belief in miracles. There is no reason why it should work, when for a period of anywhere from hours to days nothing has worked, but there actually have been a few times when it has. The mere routine of consciously "re-enacting the crime," so to speak, of deliberately attempting to do again precisely what I have done on some previous occasion, has now and then, though admittedly very rarely, made some poor fish volunteer to serve as stand-in for that other fish that I once caught with that same cast of that same fly in that same spot. Maybe it has something to do with an unwitting resurgence of that feeling Theodore Gordon categorized in his dictum: "Cast your fly with confidence."

Much more often, of course, and in fact typically, nothing at all will happen after you've gone through this elaborate reinvocation of the past, and you must resort to some other mental accompaniment to your continuing casting. So you start thinking about this fly you're using (or if that's just a dull drab nameless blob of fur or dubbing, then about this rod, or this reel, or this line or this leader) and where you got it, and who else you know who has one just like it, or where you've been when you've used it, and with whom, and what happened, or even what you've ever either read or heard about it, and before you know it you will have followed such a long trail, in this woolgathering, that you've almost forgotten where you are or what you're doing. No, you're not in anything like an actual trance, but just in pursuing a train of recollection you have shifted your concentration away from your previous intentness on the actual mechanics of what you were doing. You may, for instance, have neglected to retrieve your fly in quite as businesslike a manner as before.

This happened to me one of those afternoons in the doldrums, not long ago. I was fishing a fly, to no response whatever, when it occurred to me that I'd forgotten what it was called. It didn't matter much because the fly was certainly doing nothing to make it memorable, but it bothered me just the same. I remembered that it was a western fly that I'd got from Peter Alport, and I thought it was called a Humpy but that it was a near twin of another western fly that had an unusual name—some sort of bug. The only bug I could think of was the Zug Bug, which I've used much more frequently than this relatively exotic number from Norm Thompson out on the coast. Bug, bug, a something bug, not a Zug Bug . . .

I even remembered using it once out west while fishing the Firehole in Yellowstone Park with Russ Peak, the Stradivarius of the glass rod, and remembering that I took a hell of a good brown on it, and how embarrassed I was to see Russ wince as I said so—having forgotten completely, with my language as completely unbuttoned as it always is out fishing, that Russ Peak, aside from being one of the best rod makers alive, happens also to be a minister of the gospel, and what a goof I'd made. . . .

Goof! Goofus! That's the word, a Goofus Bug. That's the name for the other fly almost the same as a Humpy . . . !

In my abstraction, trying to think of a word, I'd gone through the unconscious reflex action of taking out a cigarette and lighting it, cradling my rod in my arm as I did so, and now the rod started slithering away, the line hissing and the reel whining, and there was a splash out in the middle of the spring pond as a three-pound brown cleared the water in what looked like a three-foot jump. It startled me so much that for a moment I didn't realize there was any connection between the bizarre behavior of my rod and the antics of that leaping brown, and the rod was on the ground and moving rapidly toward the edge of the mall between the ponds before I had the sense to grab it and start to play the fish.

That Goofus Bug had probably been sitting there motionless on the glassy surface for somewhere between three and five minutes before that crazy brown took it into his primitive brain to jump it. From the splash, he might even have pounced down on it from above, the way trout arc down onto a spider on the surface, before taking off in that leap he was making when I first saw him. It was only because I had become too engrossed in my thoughts and the momentary diversion of lighting a cigarette, that I had stopped giving the Goofus Bug the intermittent twitching retrieve that I always give any dry fly on our ponds, and that I had been giving it for better than an hour before that with no result whatsoever. There is virtually no current in our ponds, so any action a dry fly has on them must be imparted by the fisherman. Unless you twitch them, they just sit there utterly unanimated, totally unlike stream fishing where the current carries them along like little sailboats.

So a fishless day was redeemed, not by my efforts, but by my momentary neglect of them. The only fish I caught was on the one occasion that afternoon that I had for the moment stopped trying to catch one. Normally, I'd bet that the last way to catch a fish on one of our ponds would be to throw out a dry fly like the Goofus Bug and let it sit there for a matter of minutes.

But the perversity of fish can be likened, I think sometimes, to the perversity of cats. They won't come when you want them, but only when they're good and sure that it's their idea and not yours.

But that, too, was another abnormal break in the doldrums. What I normally do, when the ponds go so dead that I begin to feel like a becalmed sailor, is go over to a bench and spread out on it all the flies I've got on me, looking for the least likely candidate for success. Spreading them all out on the bench, I look for a fly that has never, to the best of my recollection, taken a fish—at least, for me—anywhere I've ever tried it. I figure that if the fish are now passing up every fly that is a logical choice for this time and place and season of the year, my one chance is to give them something utterly illogical, and to present it to them in as unorthodox a manner as I can dream up.

For example, one time in such a mood and such a predicament, I fished out a Strawman from a tangle of other flies. Now there, I thought, is a fly on which I've never taken a fish of any kind. Nor has Al McClane. Nor does either of us even know anybody who ever has. I remember asking Al this and his saying that he had also asked a lot of other people. Yet we both revere the memory of Paul Young, who first devised it, and that alone would be enough, you'd think, to put the Strawman in that category of flies we would "cast with confidence."

Paul Young's been gone since early '61, so this particular Strawman that I tie on now must be anywhere from twelve to fifteen years old. I remember I always fished it as a nymph, which it is, giving it the slowest of slow retrieves. I remember Paul's saying that he made it in imitation of those little straw "shacks" that the caddis flies shed, as they leave the larval stage, so obviously it isn't something that ought to go skittering around like Mehitabel but should be given as nearly no motion at all as you can possibly impart to a fly. It looks, in size and shape, about like a blackberry. He dyed them various colors, down to black, of which I remember one that was a peculiarly poisonous-looking purple, but the one I fish out now, taking a good minute and a half to unpuzzle it out of a cluster of flies with most intricately locked hooks, happens to be the natural straw color.

I decide to dap the damn thing, to give it the wildest remove from any conceivable natural behavior. I feel as foolish, for the first few minutes, as if I were plopping cherries in the pond. But as I go along the water's edge, plop·plop·plop, flailing the surface with it, I see more and more motion around it, and I keep on, working my 4¼-foot rod up and down like a pump handle, causing the twelve-foot leader to flick the fly here and there as I go, about six to seven feet out from the shore, where the water is about four feet deep. I gather, from the commotion I'm causing, that a lot of ten-to-twelve-inch trout are holding a series of meetings to consider this strangely persistent phenomenon. This is interesting in itself, not that it puts me any closer to the actual taking of a fish than I was before, when my slow retrieve of a Montana nymph was absolutely uneventful.

But stay—this next little meeting is rudely interrupted, as a mouth that could belong to a snapping turtle closes over my dapped Strawman, and a brown as long as your arm has got it and he's off with it.

But does that mean that the same thing will work again, either tomorrow or the day after? Almost certainly not, but the chances are that something else, equally unlikely, will work—that is, if anything will.

There sounds, of course, the oldest cry of the angler. The golfer knows, when he comes to play a round, that the course won't have disappeared overnight, and the tennis player knows that, whether or not his serve is working well, he'll at least get a given number of chances to use it. But for the fisherman, all too often, he makes all the requisite motions, and the result is tantamount to the frustration a golfer or a tennis player would feel if he made all the moves of his game, with all his accustomed and long-acquired skill, without a club or a racket in his hand.

There are times when, as the cartoonist Webster used to put it, a feller needs a friend. But sometimes the angler needs more than that, because friends can sometimes, with the best will in the world, take fish when you don't. It's then the angler most feels the need of a well-furnished mind into which to retreat as his one sure bastion of defense lest he see and treat his friends as his enemies.

There are many mental devices, such as counting five hundred before you let yourself say a word when you're afraid that whatever you start to say will turn into an explosion. But these are poor palliatives at best, because they provide nothing to lessen, or cushion, your mounting sense of frustration. So there really is no remedy, outside of philosophy, for the always potentially recurrent fits of fisherman's anger.

The only sure savior of sanity, I feel, is the possession of a rich enough mental store, or inventory, of thoughts or memories or associations with angling to see you through, no matter how soon or often or long the fish may be out on strike against you. You can never know when they will be. They can stop biting as suddenly and inexplicably as they begin, or even worse, they can simply refuse to start biting. When that happens, the odds are all theirs because they have more time than you have, and they have no other calls upon it. They have no appointments to keep, no deadlines to meet, no urgent duties or obligations to worry about—when you stop to think about it, don't you marvel that we ever got into the habit of referring to them as "poor fish"?

One thing that does help maintain the angler's equilibrium, I feel sure, is the realization that the experts, for all their vaunted prowess, can get just as ingloriously skunked as you can. In this sense, we are indeed all equal. But, unless you happen to be personally acquainted with some experts, I know you will find this hard to believe. We all assume the other guy knows something we don't know, and we are never content until we find it out. We can't believe that the answer is that there is no answer.

When Charlie Ritz lived over here as a young man he fished a lot, and whenever anybody on a stream asked him what he was using he'd say "Coachman," whether he was or not. He never got over being surprised at how often it worked. People would come back and thank him for the tip, until sometimes he was even impelled to put one on himself, thus finding himself in the bizarre position of accepting his own advice, even if it was on the rebound. He simply reasoned that more people know about the Coachman than any other fly and are thus more likely to have one, and that in the long run it doesn't matter much anyway, as the only fly that positively won't catch a fish is the fly that isn't in the water.

It's either this last consideration, or sheer fatalism, that impels some fishermen, every so often, to go through protracted phases of using only one fly. You get convinced that the one moment that a fish might take your fly is the one when you have it out of the water to change it for another. And if enough of them in succession don't produce a strike, then you're sure that you must have missed a lot of strikes in all that time you spent with your back turned changing flies one after another.

I know one season on the Esopus, when I was religiously keeping exact track of how many fish were taken on which flies, and at what time, on which date and under what weather conditions, etc., etc., etc., I finally got so infuriated at a prolonged spell of fishlessness after opening day that I decided to chuck the whole routine and stick to the one fly I had on, which happened to be a light Cahill size 14. By the season's end I found I had taken just about as many fish as I had the year before, when I had consistently carried close to five hundred flies in my overstuffed fishing clothes and made a conscientious effort to use them all. Still another year, after a weekend of great success with the Cahill bivisible spider size 16, I stuck to it the rest of the season and wound up doing just about the same as the other two seasons.

If you fish enough, you're going to take a certain number of fish, over a given amount of time. While this is both hard to remember and fairly poor consolation on those occasions when the fish are refusing to give you the time of day or night, it ought to be a sobering consideration in those moments of high elation in a hot spot when you can seemingly do no wrong—this is when we ought to remember, but somehow never do, that the time is surely coming when we can seemingly do no right.

There's no sure form of rainy-day insurance outside of philosophy, against the gloom of those times. Perhaps it's just as well there isn't. Maybe the one essential ingredient of angling, the one thing that insures that we'll always be back trying again, whether we come muttering or not, is its glorious uncertainty.

# The Girl and the Trout

NELSON BRYANT



One warm April afternoon many years ago an old trout and a young girl, although neither was captured, provided me with one of my most memorable angling interludes.

In the decades since that day I have caught ouananiche in Quebec and Labrador; brown trout in Scotland; bonefish in the Bahamas; tarpon off Costa Rica, Florida and Grand Cayman Island; permit off Key West; Atlantic salmon in Quebec; giant bluefin tuna and white marlin off Cape Cod; snook in the Everglades; amberjack and channel bass off Cape Hatteras; bluefish and striped bass from Maine to Virginia; barracuda off Jamaica; and a variety of fresh-water fish throughout the United States. None of these endeavors outshines that April day on Martha's Vineyard Island thirty-five years ago.

Smelt and alewives were spawning in the Vineyard's Mill Brook, red-winged blackbirds caroled from the streamside alders, and with an old but gleaming split bamboo flyrod my father had given me I was fishing for trout with spinner and worm.

I was, I regret to report, rushing the season by a week, but to a boy of fourteen the law seemed remote and a little silly. I had waited all through the long winter for that moment—waited while southerly storms threw long gray combers against the outer beach and salt spray driven far inland dried milky white on the windows of my island home.

I had thought of trout in December when I waded the same brook hunting black ducks that had sought shelter there from the wind and snow, and I had thought of trout in January when a warm wind came off the ocean and thawed the ice in the salt marshes making it possible for me to set my muskrat traps. Even then under the weak winter sun, the marsh had seemed to awaken and release an aroma that was more appealing to me than the world's most exotic spices.

And on that afternoon a week away from opening day I began to fish at the place we knew as Stepping Stones. Boulders had been set in the brook there so that one could cross dryshod from Etta Luce's meadows to the center of town without walking down the main road. Immediately below Stepping Stones was a deep pool and from it I took three native trout, all about ten inches long and deep-bellied and dark. With them in my creel I relaxed, for I had promised my mother (who in her eternal youth and understanding, which persists to this day, also felt that it was right for a boy to enjoy certain special privileges) some fresh trout for supper.

I savored every foot of the brook as if it were the noblest salmon river in the world as I moved downstream to the second pool, just above a spot where a maple sends a giant limb horizontally over the stream. I spent half an hour watching the alewives milling in the still water where they rested before they lunged upstream over the pebbly shallows where some would leave gleaming, jewel-like scales on the bottom. If one is waiting for an alewife run in a certain stream, these scales are a sure sign that the fish have passed by.

I tried to get the alewives to hit my spinner, but they would have nothing to do with it. (It was more than a quarter of a century later that I learned they would hit a tiny white fly.) This was the first spring run of these fish, and I knew they would surge up-current to the pool below the impassable Mill Pond dam. Here they would be easy game for boys with dip nets. The roe of the alewife, or herring as it is more commonly called along seacoast New England, is as much a part of spring as maple syrup in the north country. Fried in butter, it is more delicate in texture and flavor than the better-known shad roe.

Although at least a hundred alewives were in the pool, they did not disturb the trout, and four more of the latter were added to my creel before I moved on.

Fifty yards downstream a small brook from Antone Alley's cranberry bog used to enter Mill Brook. Just below that point the main stream begins to widen into what eventually becomes Town Cove, the northernmost finger of Tisbury Great Pond. The alewives had come in from the ocean through a cut in the beach three miles away, returning to the stream of their birth to spawn. A salt pond periodically opened to the sea by man when its waters become too fresh and too high, Tisbury Pond supports eels, white perch, sand dabs, flounders, silverside minnows, sand eels, shrimp, killifish, oysters, blue-claw crabs and soft-shelled clams. Striped bass occasionally enter the pond, and small bluefish, called snappers, can frequently be caught in October. Born offshore in June, the tiny blues rush inshore to the pond for sanctuary and food, and by early fall they will weigh a quarter of a pound or more.

Having reached the spot where the brook and Town Cove meet, I knew that the truly productive pools were behind me, but I always hoped that someday I would be able to catch one of the few large brook trout, often called salters, that apparently spent more time in the main body of the pond than in the brook. I knew that men seining for white perch in the upper reaches of the pond usually netted one or two huge—three-to-four-pound—brook trout each year, and it seemed possible that they would sometimes move a short distance into the brook.

Sitting on a grass-covered bank in the sun, I studied the

long eddy before me, and the only sounds were those of moving water, the blackbirds and the cry of an occasional herring gull. Ten minutes later, my reverie was shattered when a good-sized rock splashed into the brook in front of me. Two more followed before I could locate their source.

A pretty, piquant face framed in black hair smiled at me from the opposite side of the stream. It belonged to one of my classmates in school, a girl I shall call Penelope.

"Hi!" she said. "Catching anything?"

"Don't do that! You'll frighten the trout!" I responded churlishly.

She heaved three more stones, larger than the first.

"You're going to get it if you keep that up!" I growled manfully.

"Get what?" she asked with an impish grin.

Having no real idea of what she was going to get, I said nothing.

"There's a way to make me stop," Penelope said as she sat down and dangled her bare feet in the water. Her legs were scratched with briars and splotched with mud, but even so, they were nice legs.

"What's that?" I asked.

"I'll stop if you'll love me," she replied. "Love" is a euphemism for the word she used, a word I had rarely heard from a girl's lips.

It would be good for my ego, I suppose, to say that I plunged across the stream like a rampaging Cape buffalo and seized her in my arms, but that would not be true. Stunned into silence and immobility, my first thought was that she would be able to hear my heart hammering in its bony cage, and I dared not look at her.

"Well?" she asked.

I looked at the water running over the stones, examined my fingernails with minute care, adjusted my creel, watched a gull wheel by and was speechless.

Often in my wild and secret dreams at night I had enjoyed such a liaison with Penelope, but reality on a bright April afternoon was more than I could embrace. Moreover, I reasoned desperately, she was not my best girl. My best girl, whose hair was as gold as ripe corn, lived on the North Shore of the Island.

Facing Penelope for the first time since she made her proposal, I said, "I think I'll keep on fishing, but I hope you won't throw any more stones."

Her reaction was a look that held both amusement and scorn. She tossed her dark hair and left, the bushes closing behind her.

Awash with wild surmise, surprise, and, belatedly, regret, I remained where I was for half an hour. Then, the turmoil abating, I idly lowered my worm-baited spinner down the current along the west bank.

A huge, dark shape rushed out from under the undercut bank and hit my baited lure. Feeling the pressure of the line, it plowed across the shallows in front of me, its dorsal fin out of water—a brook trout that would have gone better than four pounds. In another instant, he had cleared the shallows and lunged into a tangle of roots. The line snagged, then parted, and once again I was shaking with unresolved desire.

I tried for that trout all that year but never saw him again. The following spring, some boys spearing alewives in that same area of the brook came home with a five-pound brook trout. Although it grieves me to say so, I think it was the same fish.

And what of Penelope?

Her family went off-Island a few years after our April meeting, and much later I heard that she was happily married and raising a substantial crop of children.

I wish her well, for she taught me, as did the great trout, that many of life's most evocative memories come from encounters that stop short of fruition, leaving one to speculate forever on what might have been.

# Joe Brooks in Memoriam

ED KOCH



My personal feeling is that the Lord has His own way of bestowing blessings, unexpected and undeserved as they usually are, on members of the angling fraternity. My blessing in this particular

My sincere thanks and grateful appreciation to Mary Brooks for her permission to use material from Joe's scrapbooks and memoirs dating back to the early 1930's. Also, my thanks for two days of friendship and hospitality shared with Mary in her home which my wife, JoAnn, and I shall never forget.

instance was to have known and been associated with Joe Brooks for some fifteen years as a friend and as a member of the Brotherhood of the Jungle Cock. The friendship was one of admiration and inspiration for me. However, that's getting a little ahead of the story.

It was during the last weekend of September, 1972 that Eric Peper of Field & Stream Book Club and I fished the West Branch of the Delaware in New York State. After dinner the first evening Eric told me of the plans for a forthcoming book that was to include chapters by noted authors on their one outstanding or memorable fishing experience. Joe had been invited to participate, but he had passed away before ever having an opportunity to reply. Eric asked me to consider writing something about Joe for the book. My first reaction was, "There are hundreds who could do a much better job than I."

"Yes," he replied, "but from some of the stories you have told me about him helping others through the Jungle Cock and so on, your story would be different, something many people may not even be aware of. Why don't you think about it?"

By Saturday night I had agreed, although I was still uncertain about the whole idea.

Upon returning home I was still hesitant to call or write Mary for her permission. When I finally did get around to calling her she was not only agreeable but she was also enthusiastic about the idea. She told me she had organized Joe's notes, scrapbooks and files and that I could read through these and use whatever I felt would be helpful. JoAnn and I made plans to spend several days with her in January.

Joe was the last living founder of the Brotherhood of the Jungle Cock. For a three-day "campfire" weekend each May, in the Catoctin Mountains of Maryland, this group gathers to "take at least one boy a-fishing" as the creed of the Brotherhood reads. It was during these weekend campfires that the members of the Brotherhood had an opportunity to observe and become involved with a side of Joe's life of which too few people were aware. To enlighten my readers, the following is a brief history of the Brotherhood.

The Jungle Cock really began in the spring of 1938 when Joe Brooks, then chairman of the Fresh Water Committee of the Maryland State Game and Fish Protective Association; J. Hammond Brown, president of the same organization; and Frank L. Bentz, public relations director of the Maryland Game and Inland Fish Commission planned a trout fishing party for about twenty-five men at Big Hunting Creek in Maryland. It was termed the Anglers' Campfire and was so successful that plans were made to make it an annual affair.

The first organized meeting was held in 1940. It was fostered by the Maryland State Game and Fish Protective Association and by the Outdoor Writers Association of America. Mr. Van Campen Heilner, well-known outdoor writer, was elected as the first official president. Since that time many well-known men have filled the president's chair, and the Creed has been taken from the Catoctin Mountains of Maryland to the far corners of the earth.

Originally the organization functioned without formal membership or dues, and it soon outgrew the limited facilities at Hunting Creek. Because of its high ideals and through the courtesy of Mr. Aaron Strauss, Camp Airy, just above Thurmont, Maryland, was made available for the annual get-together. The campfire gatherings have been held there ever since. In keeping with the spirit of the Creed, since 1949 the campfire has been restricted to men who either brought a boy or sponsored one. This requirement still applies, and attendance is by invitation only. The Creed is reproduced below as an example of the kind of ideal which Joe Brooks strived to instill in young men:

*Creed of the Brotherhood of the Jungle Cock*

We, who love angling, in order that it may enjoy, practice and reward in the later generations, mutually move together towards a common goal—the conservation and restoration of American game fishes.

Towards this end we pledge that our creel limits shall always be less than the legal restrictions and well within the bounty of Nature herself.

Enjoying, as we do, only a life estate in the out of doors, and morally charged in our time with the responsibility of handing it down unspoiled to tomorrow's inheritors, we individually undertake annually to take at least one boy a-fishing, instructing him, as best we know, in the responsibilities that are soon to be wholly his.

Holding that moral law transcends the legal statutes, always beyond the needs of any one man, and holding that example alone is the one certain teacher, we pledge always to conduct ourselves in such fashion on the stream as to make safe for others the heritage which is ours and theirs.

Of all Joe's dreams, goals and ambitions, the success of the Brotherhood was his fondest. He never missed a campfire except for illness. He would even plan his fishing trips around the Jungle Cock weekend in order to spend time with boys and men he enjoyed and admired. Each year he brought with him one, two, three and sometimes four boys for the weekend. They used his rods, reels, lines, nets, flies and anything else he felt they needed to be encouraged to continue in their pursuit of the love of angling.

Joe never ceased talking of the pleasure he saw in the faces of the boys year after year as they returned and became accomplished fly fishermen. He was forever amazed at the number of boys who started at age ten or twelve to attend Jungle Cock and by the time they'd reached fifteen or sixteen were acting as junior instructors in various classes for the younger boys.

Everyone knew of Joe as a world-famous angler, conservationist, and outdoor writer, but far too few were privileged to know him as the gentle and unselfish man he really was. The men and boys who attended campfire weekends were privileged indeed.

I was elected president of the Brotherhood for 1972–73. What a privilege to hold such an honored office; privileged to be able to relate to anglers the world over of Joe's inspiration through our association with boys.

Joe's love for youngsters goes back many years. In the late 1930's and early 1940's he was active in the Maryland State Game and Fish Protective Association. He, along with others, was responsible for starting their junior membership group. Joe edited a small pamphlet entitled "The Junior Outdoorsman." Yes, early in the game, he enjoyed writing stories that would encourage young people to get involved in the out of doors. His writing in that little journal reflected the values for which he stood: respect for the land, for the fruits of the land, and for other people. The following poem from the second issue shows this better than I can tell it.

*If We Had A Boy*

*If we had a boy, I would say to him, "Son!*
*Be fair and be square in the race you will run;*
*Be brave if you lose. Be meek if you win.*
*Be better and nobler than I've ever been."*

*I would tell him of things that are wicked and bad.*
*For I figure such knowledge should come from his Dad.*
*I would teach him and show him the best that I could,*
*That it pays to be honest, upright and good.*

*If we had a boy, I would want him to know*
*"You reap in this world just about as you sow,*
*And you get what you earn, be it little or great,*
*Regardless of luck and regardless of fate.*

*"Then, borrow no money and pay as you go,*
*Reward your true friends. Be kind to your foe.*
*To all of your promises, strive to be true,*
*And honor the name we've given to you."*

Earlier I mentioned that Joe brought several boys to the campfire meetings of the Jungle Cock. One boy in particular will live in my memory forever. He was a neighbor of Joe's and Mary's by the name of Marvin. Joe brought Marvin to the Campfire when he was about twelve. I never saw a lad so turned on by fishing. He learned to fly-cast and to tie flies as eagerly as a young setter pup takes to his first covey of quail. In four short years he was an instructor in the fly tying, fly casting and streamside classes. Every year Joe supplied Marvin's equipment for the weekend.

Marvin graduated from high school, entered college and missed several campfires because of exams. When he did return he jumped right in and worked as hard as, in fact harder than, some of the adult instructors. He could never do enough. This time Marvin had brought a friend with him, and Joe had brought another youngster along.

Marvin entered medical school and missed a few more campfires. One day I received a letter from him. He was getting married in the summer and he planned to spend several days fishing the Yellow Breeches in Pennsylvania with his wife on their honeymoon! He asked if I could fish with them. Gladly, I replied.

He and his bride showed up and I met them in the meadow at Allenberry. As they donned their fishing gear I got the shock of my life. Marvin had on a pair of Joe's waders, and he was using Joe's vest, rod, reel and line. His wife had an outfit of Mary's.

Marvin was working his way through med school, and funds were too tight to buy even inexpensive tackle—so Joe had come to his aid again, ten or twelve years after Marvin's first Jungle Cock weekend. This is the kind of guy Joe was.

Another young man comes to mind, and this one much closer to home. A young lad named Tony Skilton first attended the Jungle Cock with me at age twelve. In his wildest dreams he never expected to meet Joe Brooks face to face. Well, he not only met Joe, but ate breakfast with him, fished with him and talked with Joe for hours on end. Tony lived for the campfire weekends and the opportunity to spend time with Joe.

Tony had tied flies for me to earn spending money when I had a tackle shop in Carlisle, Pa. One weekend at the Campfire Joe asked him to tie an order of flies for him to take to Montana. Tony was on cloud nine for months after that.

The summers passed, and Tony wanted to go to college. Money was tight, and he knew he would have to work to pay his way. One night after the younger boys were in bed, Joe and I sat talking in the dining hall at camp, and I mentioned Tony's plans for school. Immediately Joe replied, "Why doesn't he tie flies to help pay his way? He's one of the best young fly tiers I've seen in a long time."

"Great," I said, "but for whom?"

"Orvis is always in need of good tiers," he returned. "I'll write to Orvis and recommend Tony. You used to tie flies for them. Why don't you write to them yourself?"

Joe had Tony tie some samples that weekend, and he sent them along with his letter. Needless to say, Tony got a job. He paid his way through college tying flies, and he even worked for Orvis two summers. The rest is history. Tony has now been on the Orvis staff for three years, and he's doing a great job. No one was happier for Tony than Joe Brooks.

One of the few times Joe ever missed the Jungle Cock campfire was the year he was in the Mayo Clinic with back trouble. That weekend the Brotherhood sent Joe a get-well card along with a list containing the names of the four hundred men and boys in camp that spring. Joe had kept the card and list in one of his scrapbooks.

Mary related another story over coffee one evening that deserves telling. A mutual friend and fishing companion from the Brotherhood had suffered a stroke some years before that had left him almost totally incapacitated. Every month, once a month, no matter where he was, Joe would call the man on the telephone and just talk with him even though his friend could not speak. Whenever they were in the area Joe and Mary would take the time to drive and visit our friend for several hours. Again, that was the Joe Brooks I was fortunate enough to know.

It was an awe-inspiring experience on January 23, 1973, to sit in Joe Brooks' den with my wife, JoAnn, and Mary and thumb through Joe's scrapbooks, files and papers that spanned some forty years. Even more inspiring was to sit at Joe's desk and make preparatory notes for this chapter.

Joe had been my idol in early years, later my friend and sometimes my fishing companion. Yet, I never dreamed that I would one day be sitting at his desk attempting to write an article in memory of him. It was difficult, to say the least.

My mind wandered and flashed back to scenes of Campfire weekends: Joe taking boys streamside to fish, teaching them to cast, giving fly-tying lessons, watching movies with the boys at the end of a long day. There was so much to remember now even though I only saw Joe once or twice a year. Tears came to my eyes occasionally as I sat reading letters Mary received from friends and acquaintances the world over. Some had met Joe only one time, perhaps for an hour or less, but the experience of spending any amount of time with Joe left an impact that they would carry with them the rest of their lives. Not because he was great or world-renowned but because he was a delightful, everyday, down-to-earth person.

He was sincere, genuine, kind and interested in passing on

to others the joy he found in his own angling experience. He was never too busy to help a young lad he found wandering streamside or to spend hours in the evening discussing conservation plans to improve fishing. Whenever or wherever he found an active or interested group of conservationists he was willing to jump in and get involved. Many a Friday or Saturday night at the Campfire the sessions went to the wee hours of the morning. With only a few hours' sleep Joe would show up for breakfast with his boys ready to hit the stream.

As a final tribute to Joe, Mary gave her permission* to print portions of letters she had received. These are, I want to add, just a few of the hundreds I was able to read in one short evening. They tell far better than I could ever do just how people thought about Joe.

*From a news column*

Joe Brooks: Legend and Legacy

*October 4, 1972*

I did not know Joe well, but what I do know about him is—I believe—worth telling.

A couple of days after Christmas, 1962, I drove to Joe's home in Richmond, Va. I was twenty-two years old and I knew I wanted to be an outdoor writer. That's about all I knew. Through a mutual friend, I had made an appointment to meet Joe and get some advice on how to start a career.

I was surprised that he would even consent to talk with me, and quite frankly, I expected him to be a stuffed shirt. I could hardly have been more mistaken. For several hours, Joe took valuable time off from his writing to help me chart a career. He showed me his gear, his photo files, his book collection. His wife,

*In accordance with Mary Brooks' wishes, we have not given the full names of her correspondents. However, we can assure you that you would recognize the names of several of the letter writers as outdoor writers to whom Joe Brooks provided either inspiration, guidance or both.

Mary, brought us coffee. I was impressed with his gentleness and obvious interest in getting me off on the right foot.

Although we have written each other occasionally in the past decade, I only saw him once more. That was in Thurmont, Maryland, where Joe was attending an annual meeting of the Brotherhood of the Jungle Cock—an organization which he and some of his friends started many years ago. Characteristically, it is devoted to teaching kids—especially underprivileged kids—the joys of trout fishing.

Despite Joe's legendary status, I saw him spend hours teaching wide-eyed kids how to catch fish. He had the patience of Job, and obviously enjoyed the experience as much as the kids.

Joe's personal approach to fishing was like his approach to life. He savored the present and took what enjoyment the day had to offer. You'd think that a man who had fished all over the world—tarpon in Florida, trout in Chile, salmon in Europe—would be bored with the eight-inch trout in North Carolina's small mountain streams. Not so. When Joe visited the Tarheel State some years back, he stalked our little trout with the same zeal he sought ten-pound browns in South America or New Zealand.

Joe's career is all the more remarkable because of a major obstacle he overcame early. A native of Baltimore, Joe often remarked that he was an alcoholic. He was not ashamed of it. In his youth, he was a heavy drinker, but he dragged himself out of the gutter and never touched another drop for nearly forty years. He was no prude about alcohol, but he knew he would never again be able to drink.

Perhaps as much as anything, this shows the moral fiber and gentle decency of the man. His victory over alcohol and the remarkable career that followed stand as a challenge and guide for us all—fishermen and non-fishermen alike.

He taught most of us how to fish, but he also showed us how to live.

*From a Letter to Mary Brooks*

*October 19, 1972*

Dear Mary,

I must keep this brief, lest I write on many pages. When Doug wrote me about Joe passing away, I must tell you that I didn't feel like doing much for a day or two—thank heavens I had plenty to do here at the St. John's Military Academy where I am teaching and coaching. I know that you must be deluged with letters expressing condolences, but let me add that no man impressed me more than your husband. It was his kind note that he slipped on the window-catch of my trailer on Rock Creek back in 1968, just after being appointed *Outdoor Life* fishing editor, that really gave me the impetus to go ahead and give outdoor writing a real try. Up to that time, I had never published a magazine story. Now, I have twenty, including two in *Outdoor Life.* I believe that I am not that good a writer, and you must understand that inspiration that I find from influences like Joe has been an immeasurable spark to me. . . .

Joe said that he would review my first attempt at a trout fishing article, which had been in a Wisconsin newspaper. Well, though I talked with you folks at the Lodge, I never showed up for that discussion because I turned scared: who was I to take up the time of Joe Brooks. It was a day later that I found a note stuck in the corner of the window of my travel trailer at the Elkhorn Ranch, four miles up dusty, rutted Rock Creek Road. It seems ironic now that the note is misplaced, though I have thought of it often when I get bogged down in my writing—which is almost always. Joe wrote something about "Keep on trying, and you'll do fine, Best Wishes—Joe Brooks." You know, in the few times I saw you people since that day, I don't ever remember asking Joe if he had driven up to the trailer and placed the note there while I was out fishing. . . .

*From a Letter to Mary Brooks*

*Sept. 25, 1972*

Dearest Mary,

By far this is the most difficult thing that I have ever had to write in my entire life. Mary and I are shocked and deeply grieved upon returning from a fishing trip and learning of your tragedy.

I need not tell you that we share with you these difficult days. Joe provided the inspiration that I so badly needed as a struggling writer many years ago and I shall be ever grateful for his encouragements and guidance that proved to be so helpful.

It must be a great pride to know that Joe attained the very highest degree of stature in the outdoors field. His great articles and books well serve as great inspirations and fulfull many pleasurable hours of reading for generations to come. This is a mark that few individuals can ever hope to attain.

If in the remaining years of my life I can attain even a small portion of such achievements as did Joe, I will be a very pleased person.

Mary and I and the children send you our love and our prayers . . . and you know that our home is yours should you decide to get away for a while. You're always our most welcomed guest anytime.

With love and understanding,



*The following letter was written to Joe by a boy he had taken to the Jungle Cock*

*May, 1966*

Dear Mr. Brooks,

I again want to express my appreciation for your sponsoring me to the Jungle Cock meeting last weekend. It was both an honor and a pleasure to return this year and I enjoyed every minute of it. I learned quite a bit more about fly tying from Ed

Koch and about fly casting from your demonstration. I was, in turn, able to help other boys with their tying and casting. This in itself was gratifying. This year I felt as though I were a part of the Brotherhood. I have watched it grow for the past four years and I can already see the tremendous job it has thus far completed. It is a pleasure to be associated with an organization that's chief purpose is to train boys to be more worthy inheritors of the treasure nature has to offer. Thanks again for a wonderful trip.

Your fishing friend,
Marvin

*From a Letter to Mary Brooks*

Dear Mary,

I learned of Joe's death Wednesday. The news was late to reach me because I have just entered another phase of training.

There is very little one person can do to ease the pain of another in moments like these. However, I would like to share some experiences to show how Joe's life affected mine.

When Joe first responded to my request to meet him I was sixteen years old. Now I'm nearly twenty-four. A lot has happened in the intervening years and, in large degree, what has happened has been centered around Joe.

During these years Joe was very generous. He provided me with tackle and gave me opportunities to fish and write. As appreciative as I am of these gifts, there were other gifts, intangible, more valuable than these. . . .

And Joe was strong. I remember several years ago when Joe was having extreme back pain at the meeting of the Brotherhood of the Jungle Cock. Kids crowded around to tell Joe about their new fly rods, to ask him what fly they should use on Big Hunting Creek, and to request Joe to autograph their programs. No one noticed when Joe turned his head aside to swallow painkillers. No one seemed to notice the tightness in his neck as his teeth clenched behind his smile. Joe smiled, autographed and answered. He never mentioned the pain.

And Joe was a teacher. His interest in the Brotherhood of

the Jungle Cock never flagged. His articles and books always stressed conservation, stream etiquette, and the "how to." And I remember the many long discussions we had in the downstairs study and in Will's shop. Joe constantly emphasized the importance of helping others, instructed me to write, write, write and always the encouragement, the ever so helpful encouragement.

Joe was a great fisherman. He was an even greater person. It is as a person that I remember Joe. I remember him as the man who helped me become who I am, and as the person who helped many others. I am thankful to have known such a fine man.

I would like to wish you every help as you overcome your sorrow and make plans for the future. I will keep in touch over the coming months. If there's anything at all that I can do to be of help, please let me know.

I must end this letter as all others,

Thanks,
Bert

*From a Letter to Mary Brooks*

Dear Mary,

I have just received a letter telling me of Joe's death. I need not tell you that I was overwhelmed. It is hard to believe that I will never see Joe again. We were always hoping that he would come down here again.

It will never be the same any more to make a fishing trip and to know that Joe will not be there with me, that I will not even be able to write to him about the fish I have caught. He had a very rare quality which was the cleanliness of spirit of a child. In all the trips I made with him, which were many, I never heard him utter an unkind word.

I can imagine, dear Mary, your grief at having lost him and I hope you don't find it unseemly that I shed a few not unmanly tears for a friend I loved. Carole joins me in sending her sincerest regrets.

With love
Bebe

What more can I add to expressions as those? Nothing except to add that my "Moment of Truth" came to pass with the writing of this chapter in memory of Joe!

# The Happenings

ART FLICK



During the several years I worked as a guide for the Westkill Tavern Club in New York's Catskill Mountains, I met a wide variety of people. One of the finest gentlemen I met and one whom I enjoyed serving over the years was James Davies, a good sportsman and a fine fisherman with a great sense of humor. Because we were together so much over the years, our relationship was more a friendship than that of a "sport" and his guide. I'd like to share with you some of the high points of our relationship, and you can see if you agree with my feelings about Jim Davies.

You have heard of people who were accident-prone; this was not Jim's problem, but he did seem to be what I called "happening prone." When Jim was along, odd or amusing things happened. I still chuckle over these occurrences even though many years have intervened.

There was the day on the Schoharie when the March Browns, *Stenonema vicarium,* were due to emerge: it was a miserable day, one when only fools would venture forth, but Jim was as crazy as I (or vice-versa!). The wind was blowing like "Billy-be-damned," and the temperature was in the low 40's. Because the emergence time of the March Browns is sporadic, the only way one can be reasonably sure to catch the hatch is to fish all day. This being the case, we had taken our lunch with us to avoid being caught off the stream when the hatch and the feeding started.

Nothing had happened up to midday when we got together, so we decided to take our lunches down to the stream where we could watch the water. We crossed the stream to a spot we knew generally held some good fish and where we could see any insect activity that might commence. The place we chose was well downstream, just above the village of Prattsville, where there is a lovely pool.

A good portion of the flow in this pool is alongside a tremendous boulder that creates a beautiful run on its far side. Because of the way the stream flows, an eddy is formed on the near side of the boulder (where we were sitting), and the water flows in a circular fashion with only the slightest movement. Below the boulder there is a very deep hole which makes wading impossible.

In consideration of the low temperature, we gathered some driftwood and made ourselves a nice fire and proceeded to eat our sandwiches and drink our coffee. Sometime after we finished lunch, a few flies began to appear. The air was so cold, however, that few if any of the flies became airborne—they were practically paralyzed! With the wind blowing hard from the northwest, many of them were being blown on the surface toward us and those that wound up in the eddy just drifted around. It wasn't long before we had quite a collection of the meaty creatures in front of us.

There were no fish rising, but suddenly Jim asked, "Art, have you ever tried chumming for trout?" Naturally I said that I'd never heard of such a thing and that I wanted to know just exactly how one would go about doing it. Jim replied, "What do you suppose would happen if we drifted a whole mess of those flies down the run along the rock where there are usually some good fish? If George La Branche could create a hatch with artificial flies, we darn sure ought to be able to create one by floating a bunch of naturals over them."

I didn't know what would happen, but being the guide, I took the hint and gathered up a mess of the flies in my hat. I walked to the head of the run and proceeded to drop flies so they would float over the places we expected trout to be.

The first lot went down with no takers, but with nothing better to do, I gathered up some more and started drifting them down, too. Much to my surprise, first one and then two or three fish started feeding on them with the noisy splashes that feeding rainbows make.

I called to Jim to get to work, so he got up, picked up his rod that had been standing in the willows, and moved upstream into a position where he could drift a fly down to the feeding fish. This was the only way the fish could be reached because of the depth of the water below. With care one could float a fly over their lie nicely—we had often done it in the past by leaving enough slack line so the fly would drift over them naturally.

Jim made his cast nicely, and the fly floated perfectly over the nearest riser. The fish came up and took the fly with a splash. Jim reared back and of course the leader parted. Always the sympathetic gentleman, I laughed loud and long. While Jim was walking back to the fire, he said, "All right, wise guy, let's see if you can do any better."

These were the days before nylon leaders and we should have known better than to fish with a gut leader that had been standing out in the wind for over a half hour. Gut that dry was practically useless. Even if Jim didn't think of it, I certainly should have.

Like Jim I went upstream into position to drift my fly down to the other feeding fish. Unfortunately for me the second fish rose in the same manner, and although I did raise my rod fairly gently, my performance was a repeat of Jim's. At this point, Jim gave out with a roar. Figuring he was giving me some of my own medicine, I turned toward him to make some wisecrack, but then I saw that he was trying to beat his burning waders. Yes, he'd moved too close to the fire and the howl was from the heat on his fanny rather than from giving me the business.

Thus ended our one and only attempt at putting out a chum line for trout.

Back in the 1940's the Schoharie and Gilboa Reservoir, into which it flows, had a good population of large rainbows up to five pounds and more. Wonderful sport could be had if a fisherman was lucky enough to find these fish feeding in the run that formed the last pool above the reservoir. Few of the big fish were reduced to possession by Jim and me, but it was exciting fishing. We would have been more successful fishing for them with wet flies and heavier tackle, but Jim was a dry fly purist.

When feeding on mayflies those fish always fed with gusto; their splashing looked more like kids playing in the water. They were extremely selective and would not take a fly presented on a leader larger than 4X—and remember those were the days of gut leaders. The result was that nine times out of ten those dogs would hit in the fast run where you could seldom follow your fly, and fast reflexes would have you rear back and, of course, pop the tippet; if, in fact, the fish had taken your fly. On the rare occasion when you did things right and hung one, it would take off for the reservoir and, without so much as a goodbye, break you. Sure, we would take some of the smaller fish, but we were always pretty certain of "getting away" from the dogs.

One evening, the fish did not start their splashy feeding until nearly dark. As the moon came up from behind the mountain and shone down on that fast riffle, it was a sight to behold. We always had trouble enough in the daylight, but with those fish beating the water to a froth and not knowing if a fish was taking a natural or our fly, all we did was break off fly after fly. After about fifteen minutes of it, Jim said, "Art, what the hell are we doing here making damned fools of ourselves? You know as well as I do we'll never stay with one of those slobs under these conditions—let's go home and have a drink." I said amen to that.

Early the following week, Jim phoned and said he had found the answer to our problem in *Field & Stream* magazine. He asked me to make him up a couple of twelve-foot leaders and

said he wasn't going to tell me what the trick was, because he didn't want me laughing at him over the phone.

He arrived Thursday afternoon, in time for the evening fishing, of course, and showed me the article. It dealt with our problem all right, and I thought it made some sense. The writer suggested one take a medium-size rubber band and, using it doubled, fasten one end to the loop in the fly line. The other end was fastened to the leader loop. The rubber band was supposed to absorb the shock of the strike, and the tippet would be less apt to break.

We strung up a rod, hooked up the rubber band, which was about an eighth of an inch wide, and tested it on the lawn. We tried putting what seemed to be about as much pull on it as we assumed a sizable trout would, and everything held together. Jim figured if he could handle a fly with the contraption he might not lose so many flies and tippets and might even stay in contact with one of the dogs.

When we got to the stream Jim found that with a bit of practice he could get his fly out fairly well. Shortly afterward a few fish started working. The next thing I knew he called to me to come over. He had a fish on, and although it wasn't one of the big ones, it looked as though the rubber band idea might work. He wanted me to take the rod to get the "feel" of it, and it *was* a different feeling. When the fish started to run, you could feel the elastic stretch before the line began to pay out. After I handed the rod back to him, Jim netted a nice fifteen-inch rainbow, and he thought the idea might work on a big one.

It didn't take long for him to find out. He tied into one of the bruisers, and, by gosh, he *didn't* break his tippet; however, the rubber band broke and he lost not only his tippet but a brand new twelve-foot leader plus his fly. You older fishermen will recall that in those days a good twelve-foot gut leader cost at least $1.25.

That was the end of the rubber band "happening."

One of Jim's favorite spots on the Schoharie was known as the Greenhouse Pool. It was a terribly deceiving piece of water and had two monstrous boulders in it; one at the head of the pool, the other halfway down and a bit to the right side of the stream. Both were known as good lies for browns, but the water near the lower boulder was the tougher of the two spots to fish properly. Fishermen in the know always approached the holding water near the lower rock from the right side of the stream. Although the rock was almost as long as a car, not much of it was above water when the stream was normal.

The Catskills start coming to life around Decoration Day, and a boarding house, located fairly close to the Greenhouse Pool about opposite the lower rock, was well tenanted with weekenders—not the fishing type. I had been fishing downstream from Jim and was about to pick him up. As I got close to his spot, I saw a large group of people on the edge of the road adjacent to the pool jabbering away and gesticulating. Of course I wondered what was up. I saw Jim had not drowned, for he was standing on the rock, holding his net, and looking at it.

When I got out of the car, I asked the closest person to me what the commotion was all about. I started to get at least six different answers all at the same time, none of which I could understand, for with the number of people all talking at once I was lost. However, I did decipher something to the effect that the man fishing on the rock had a big fish on his *pole,* but his net made him lose it. If I'd had a sound camera along, it would have made a priceless recording.

I called to Jim and asked what was going on. He let his net drop back and waved his hand to me in disgust. He crossed over to my side, and we sat on a large flat rock and lit up, and I listened to this tale of woe.

"Art, of all the years I've been fishing with you, I've never stayed with a big trout—two- or three-pounders, yes, but never a fish over three pounds. While I was fishing the lower part of the pool, working upstream as usual, I saw the fish break up by the lower rock. I knew it was a larger fish than any I'd seen feeding since I had a rod on Ed Hewitt's Neversink water. I very carefully worked my way up and sized up his feeding lie, watching him take flies regularly. In due time, I put my fly over him and damned if he didn't slurp it right in, taking it with no fuss at all, so that I didn't hit him hard. Everything from then on went my way. So I'd have better control of my feet, I stepped up on the big rock that was partially out of water. Didn't want those slippery stones on the creek bottom to foul me up. Everything you'd ever taught me went through my head, because I sure didn't want to lose this baby. I had gathered quite an audience on the road, and I got to thinking you'd be proud of me the way I was handling this lovely, which was larger than anything I'd seen in the stream aside from the big downstream rainbows. For once in my life, I took it easy and didn't even think of the net until the fish turned up. I thought I was giving the spectators a darn good show and finally very carefully positioned my net in the water and led the fish into it; I even remembered to ease him in headfirst. It was a proud moment, and then I raised the net and fish, lifting them so that the people could get a good look at it. All that happened was the bottom of the net fell apart, too rotten to hold four pounds of brown trout, and of course he came unstuck and went downstream. What a helluva thing to happen."

At the moment, I doubt I'd ever felt so badly about a trout lost by a fishing companion.

Jim didn't have to be on the Schoharie to have things "happen." One year he very kindly invited me to accompany him to York's Camps, on Kennebago Lake, Maine. Because he wanted to go in late September, I could get away. Our trout season at that time closed on August 31, and the grouse season didn't open until October. Of course I accepted with pleasure. The trip to Maine would be a new experience for me as I'd never fished for squaretails or landlocks in a lake. Jim had been advised by friends that the time to fish in Maine with dry flies (he never fished anything else) was early autumn when the nights were cold, and the fish became interested in surface food.

If ever there was a character, it was Mr. York the owner. Guest or no guest, you never had to wonder what he was thinking. To say he was outspoken was putting it mildly. He welcomed us and checked with us to find what we wanted in the way of a boat, motor, guide, etc. Jim asked me if I thought we needed a guide, but I felt that because we were going to fish on top, we could see fish if they worked at all. Jim asked Mr. York if we would be able to get a guide later if we found we couldn't do anything alone. He assured us that it didn't make a damn bit of difference to him, we could have one anytime, just so long as he knew ahead.

Our first day out was a gorgeous one with hardly any wind; perfect for our kind of fishing. It had frozen during the night, and there was a very light skim of ice on the bit of water in the boat. We left the dock, and I rowed very slowly, not far from shore, past the camps. Not far ahead I saw a stream flowing into the lake. Everything I'd read told me fish in lakes have an affinity for areas where streams flow in, so I suggested to Jim that we anchor in that vicinity and watch. At that point we were not much over a quarter mile from the dock.

Jim spotted a dimple fairly close by, and a couple of fish began to feed. I suggested we try both Dun and Gray Fox variants. Both had proved successful anywhere my friends and I had used them. I doubt if two men ever had a finer day than we did. We caught brookies up to two pounds, and Jim took one landlock that weighed about four pounds. Actually, we got tired of catching fish and returned all but two which we kept to eat. We knew several women from the camps were watching us but thought nothing of it, assuming they were "fishermen's widows" who were just bored. We headed back to the dock with the pleasant thought of a couple of cold Scotches.

Mr. York was there to greet us and said some of the ladies had told him we were catching a lot of fish. We gave him a complete report, and when we told him we'd caught them all on dry flies, he allowed he'd be damned. He then asked us if he could request a favor. We agreed readily, and he asked if we would be kind enough to come down to the dock when the guides and their "sports" came in. We had no idea what he wanted, but we said we'd be there.

While we were sitting in our cabin enjoying our libations and rehashing the day's events, a knock came at the door and a voice told us Mr. York would appreciate it if we'd come down to the dock. When we got there he had his guides lined up. They apparently had not done well on wet flies or on the usual streamers, and all had motored well down the lake. Mr. York asked us if we would be good enough to relate our experience.

Well, Jim and I felt like a couple of heels, of course, but what could we do? Even though we toned it down as much as we could, it was obvious that the guides were mighty unhappy. Then, adding insult to injury, the old boy started to chew them out like I've never seen a bunch of men dressed down. The thing that seemed to bother him most was that not one of them had had brains to learn to fish with dry flies, and that it took a couple of outsiders to show them up. He yapped at them for running their boats way to hell and gone to the other end of the lake where they caught practically nothing, while we, a couple of greenhorns fishing it for the first time, had caught all kinds of fish just a short distance from camp. To say we were embarrassed is supreme understatement.

That evening at dinner Mr. York informed the other fishermen that he had ordered some dry flies flown in from Portland for those who wanted to try them. You can imagine how unpopular we were with the guides for the balance of our stay. Being a guide myself, I felt pretty lousy about it.



I couldn't help but think that even away from home, things "happened" to Jim. If he is in heaven where he deserves to be, I wonder if he also has "happenings" there?

Of one thing you can be sure, I am happy that I *happened* to become acquainted with him.

*The west is flaming in gold and purple,*
*ready for the ceremony of the sunset.*

JOHN MUIR

# Moment of Truth on the McKenzie

V. S. HIDY



To boat and fish Oregon's McKenzie River on a clear summer day is a grand experience for a trout fisherman who likes to cast a fly. Compared to our usual habit of hiking and wading a mile or two of river in an afternoon and evening, this is a leisurely approach. The guide skillfully maneuvers the boat and does all the work while you and your companion take turns catching trout. In this manner you easily cover twelve or fourteen miles of water in a day, even though you linger at those pools where the trout are most responsive to the pattern and presentation of your fly.

The voyage gives you a generous panorama of the upper ridges of the Cascade Mountains, including giant rock formations poised above miles of rolling forests beneath gargantuan white cumulus clouds. At your elbow are sheer cliffs gnawed eternally by the river and open glades with meadows of sweetbrier and daisy where the breezes smell of violets, mint and honeysuckle. Blue columbine and marsh marigolds bloom along the wet banks of the river. As you float along, harlequin ducks, hooded mergansers, orioles, water ouzels and kingfishers fly across the river or through the arbors among the trees. Lunch is eaten in the shade on a sandbar beside currents of turquoise blue. The guide prepares an ambrosia of trout over a driftwood fire while you chill a bottle of white wine in the cold water.

The fame of the McKenzie rests upon more than scenery, birds and trout. You are challenged and seduced with a magnificent variety of water full of surprise. Stay alert, the action can be fast. As you roller-coaster the rapids, the guide at the oars will shout: "Ready now! Right behind that boulder. There!" And he is usually right. A short, accurate cast in such spots will often produce a desirable trout.

At the end of the rapids you may pause to fish the pocket water among polished boulders encircled with runnels of foam. From these you float jauntily down shaded or sunswept riffles. These take you into pools and flats where great beds of moss or aquatic grasses cover the bottom. Here, unpredictably, may be more surprises—mysterious shadows, including trout, flickering and flashing over long, curving ledges of white, gray or multicolored rock. Over these moss beds, grasses and ledges, you must cast rather far. Then you give your line a tug to refloat your fly. With this maneuver you have a perfect, drag-free float with the boat and your fly moving at precisely the same speed. McKenzie River trout do not take a fly that drags—unless they are having an orgy and, Heaven forbid, you are using a dropper fly.

The dropper fly led to my most memorable experience on the McKenzie when I was fishing with three native Oregonians—Judge James W. Crawford, Dale LaFollette and Thomas Tongue, all excellent fishermen with a total experience of some fifty or sixty years on this river. I was, therefore, fishing unfamiliar waters with three anglers who knew the river well.

We had reservations for the night upstream at Cedarwood Lodge in a weathered but comfortable cabin at the river's edge. The stage setting was deceptively peaceful. There I was to be caught in the crosscurrents of some surprising testimony.

Tom and I were fishing partners for the day and we took turns catching fish. There were several lulls, of course, as well as periods of considerable action. As I recall, Tom caught a trophy trout over sixteen inches and returned it to the river according to one of the laws regarding the McKenzie. The most violent action came toward the end of the day on the pool at Byerly's Flat where the quicksilver currents mirrored the purple, orange and golden colors of sunset.

A great hatch was starting as we arrived, and the guide steered the boat under the trees to avoid disturbing the water. As Tom made his first cast, there was a frenzy of swirls, dimples and splashes. It was an orgy. The trout began to gorge themselves on thousands of hatching caddis flies.

While Tom played his first trout I tied on a dropper fly with the hope of catching doubles. On my first cast a trout took the tail fly and pulled the dropper fly beneath the water. After I set the hook, the rod dipped sharply as a second fish succeeded in catching the dropper fly.

Netting doubles is even more fun than hooking them. As my second pair of trout swerved and jumped, sometimes leaping into the air simultaneously, Tom asked the guide to tie a dropper fly to his leader.

For almost an hour we enjoyed hooking and netting doubles. Two of these rainbows would total two or three pounds, and it was a delightful climax to my first boat trip on the McKenzie.

As we drove up the river to the Lodge later, I listened to Tom, Dale and the Judge eulogize the McKenzie as the perfect trout stream for fly fishing. Those who enjoyed it were obliged, therefore, to attend it with vigilance and keep the rules of conduct unmistakably clear.

"We are all observers and guardians of these traditions," the Judge said, "And this is entirely in keeping with the character of this great river. It is important that some of us make a special effort to observe and report on the conduct of fishermen, especially those in the category of what I like to call 'borderline' sportsmen. Damned embarrassing sometimes. On a beautiful river like this!"

When we arrived at the cabin, Dale built a fire in the great stone fireplace, and I brought in a pitcher of spring water. There were ice cubes and a choice of Scotch or bourbon as we relaxed before the fire and exchanged fish stories in that carefree manner fishermen assume after they have enjoyed a perfect day. You can still feel the thud of the boat against the rocks in the riffles, hear the swishing of your line and the splashing fish at the net. You remember the first few moments of anxious navigation in the rapids and that wonderful giddy feeling as you raced along the white water with the whole world moving madly out of control.

Suddenly the fireplace exploded with a loud cannon shot and a shower of sparks as Tom announced to Dale and the Judge, "I am sorry to report that my fishing partner finished up his day on the river using live bait!"

The McKenzie murmured at the door and another shot sounded from the fireplace. The Judge calmly replenished his drink and pondered this defamatory statement by his trusted friend, attorney Thomas Tongue, who became, some years later, a justice of the Supreme Court of Oregon.

"If this accusation is true," the Judge declared, "We have here a very serious charge involving unsportsmanlike conduct. Was it a source of embarrassment to you, Tom, to witness the use of bait by a so-called fly fisherman?"

"Indeed it was. This is no borderline case, your honor. I believe the river and the fish will need some additional protection if such attacks continue."

"Did the defendant catch many trout?"

"Yes. All beautiful McKenzie rainbows."

"Does the defendant care to answer these charges at this time? The court is in session."

"Yes, your honor, I do. We were fishing there at Byerly's Flat, and the trout were so hungry they were feeding very recklessly. It was really an orgy, so I put on a dropper fly because I like to catch doubles."

"What was the pattern of the fly?"

"It was a small Bucktail Caddis tied very sparse on an extremely light wire hook, and to say that the fish enjoyed it is an understatement."

Tom interrupted my testimony. "He was catching two trout on every cast, your honor, deliberately using the first fish to activate the other fly. I consider this a vicious violation of the spirit of fly fishing."

"Objection! This is unfair to me and to the fish," I said.

"Proceed with your defense. The accusation is clear," the

Judge said. "Dale, do you agree that this is a serious charge?"

As he carefully placed another log on the fire, LaFollette said, "In my opinion, sir, this is a very serious charge."

"You have noticed, your honor, how recklessly trout will feed during a big hatch?" I asked the Judge.

"Yes, of course. It is a remarkable sight and one of the reasons some of us want to protect this river from any abuse."

"Well, I believe trout enjoy chasing these insects as they wiggle and dart to the surface and fly away. Obviously, they are happy when they catch one. Also, the fisherman is certainly happy when he feels the pull on the dropper fly. It doubles the sport. It is quite clear to me, your honor, that the dropper fly increases the pleasure of both the fish and the fishermen."

"Don't you feel any compunction at all in using this devious technique on trout that are obviously very hungry and very excited?"

"Only on one small count, sir. It does take some extra time to remove the flies and release the fish. They seem to squirm around more in the net when there are two fish side by side. This delay in getting the fish back into the water does trouble me some, but the fish are always able to swim away."

The fire was settling down. Through the door came the sounds of the river and of a hoot owl. Dale refilled all our glasses as the Judge pondered the sporting ethics of activating a fly with a fish.

After some time, the Judge rose to his feet and said, "Gentlemen, please join me in a toast to the McKenzie, a great river that has brought us together here for a most enjoyable day of fishing. It is my judgment here and now that, although the dropper fly may give extra pleasure to both the fish and the fisherman, *the use of a dropper fly should never be encouraged on any great trout stream. One trout at a time is enough.*"

To this day I have observed *Crawford's Law on the Dropper Fly* on all the rivers I have fished. There is no doubt that those who follow the law will find wisdom, and "wisdom's ways are the ways of pleasantness and all her paths are peace."

In retrospect, however, I believe the dropper fly can still be used on the McKenzie under certain conditions. We could use barbless hooks to encourage both fish to escape and we could return to the water all of the fish we catch in this manner, particularly at sunset when the trout are most active. In one sense this would circumvent *Crawford's Law.* In another sense it would be something of a tribute to the Judge, who recently passed on. Those who knew this remarkable man and cherish the memory of his devotion to the McKenzie could call this releasing of trout the Ceremony of the Sunset, in the words of John Muir. I believe it would tickle the Judge. He had a pixie sense of humor, and he approved of anything that was good for his favorite river.

# Onward and Upward

CHARLES K. FOX



If one thinks of a *fisherman,* in his pursuit of meat, as an operator from bank or boat who attempts to deceive his quarry into taking some natural bait; and if one thinks of an *angler* as a wading or boating caster who attempts to attract his quarry into seizing some artificial bait as he casts for sport, you have under consideration two entirely different types of outdoorsmen. Although it seems that the latter approach appeals more to the intellectual, there is one curious facet to it: most of the latter have at one time been the former. Therein lies a story for all fishermen and/or anglers, whether the transition be considered progression or regression. I regard my thinking-and-doing transformation as applied to fish and fishing as the most important step, literally next to walking, that I ever took; so this becomes a progress report—natural to artificial.

There are two types of incidents that excite the imagination of the angler: one is dramatic and sudden; the other is subtle and extended. It was the latter that motivated me into becoming a dedicated dry-fly fisherman for trout and salmon.

Turning back the time machine places me, a youth, in a day when few if any tapered leaders and eyed flies were available in the stores in this country. Fly rods were like the buggy whips common to that day and had flopping ring guides tied to the can. Fly-lines were light and level. The collective result of these conditions was that there was no such thing as shooting the line. It was before Hewitt and Bergman advised us how to do it. Thus, in point of time it happened that I grew up with a sport which has no peer, dry-fly fishing in America.

My Dad recognized that hunting and fishing were inbred in his firstborn and in effect he said, "It is just a matter of the form it takes, not the way it goes with that boy," and he was pleased and cooperative.

He turned me over to the best fly fisherman in the area, a man who spent much more time hunting and fishing than he did with his law practice. Sol Rupp was an innovator and an analyst, keen and skilled. He had been raised along wonderful little Cedar Run in the limestone stream section of the Cumberland Valley of Pennsylvania. He knew the brook trout native to the limestone streams, and brown trout had not yet been introduced. His inquisitive mind demanded that he now learn about equipment and how to use it. His source for both supplies and information was London, the best possible place at the time.

The first time Mr. Rupp took me fishing with him was to a beautiful mountain brooklet characterized by pools, slicks and glides and a worthy population of native brook trout. "The dry fly," he said, "is the most fun; therefore it is best."

Fascinated, I watched. A spray of crystal water tumbled into a stony basin causing a swirl. His "dry fly" landed lightly and started on a circular path in the miniature whirlpool. There

was a slash and a flash, and the fly disappeared. Possibly I was more thrilled than Mr. Rupp.

The second time out he took me to Big Spring, a limestone spring stream in a pastoral setting. "Here," he explained, "you sneak up to the trout in the clear, smooth water and you watch him as you fish for him. Over on Laurel Run you can't see the fish, you just cast into the good-looking places. It is harder to catch them here."

His fly, which he called "Light Cahill," landed above one of the better trout and drifted in a course toward him. Ever so slightly the trout rose up, inspected the fraud and settled back. I expected something else, the sort of thing that had happened on the mountain stream, so I was surprised when Mr. Rupp said with encouraging inflection, "He's interested."

Five minutes and twenty casts later I was a witness to something quite different from the Laurel Run episode. The acceptance of the fly by the trout in this situation was deliberation itself. The fish drifted with the fly, inspecting it at very close range. I saw the trout tip up, the mouth open and the fly disappear in a dainty dimple. Then I saw more. Suddenly the leader tightened and as it straightened out above the surface a tiny rainbow of spray accompanied the swish. The trout was jolted in its tracks, the gills opened with the impact and then it bolted. Again the whole affair was fascinating but ever so different from the acceptance of the fly by the mountain-stream trout.

I came to realize later that Big Spring, which flows through Newville, Pennsylvania, thirty miles from my home, was the greatest of all brook trout streams of my state. It featured a perfect balance between a high rate of natural reproduction and a great carrying capacity. In recent years the trout production of this great stream has been adversely affected by siltation from hatcheries.

Sol had learned of an English firm, Abbey & Imbrie, where he was able to purchase eyed flies and tapered Spanish silkworm gut leaders that had to be soaked and tied when wet. Fine strips of this gut, which he called "gut points," were attached to the basic leader as needed with a special "barrel knot." It was just a matter of time before Sol could secure American-made tapered lines and a split bamboo rod possessing backbone. At first these rods were called "dry fly rods." It was about this time that Eastern anglers were catching their first brown trout.

I entered Lafayette College in the fall of '27. Because this area was a hotbed of fly fishermen, the fishing tackle displays in the stores of Easton and Allentown were more impressive than anything I had yet seen. After all, the late Samuel Phillippi, who produced the first split and glued bamboo rod, was a native of Easton, and Big Jim Leisenring, the wet fly authority, was living in Allentown. Any resident of the Lehigh Valley who fly fished visited the Pocono mountain streams; the Brodhead, the Little Lehigh near Allentown and the Musconetcong and Pequest across the Delaware River in New Jersey.

Present-day fishermen will snicker about this, but at that date there were no eyed dry flies to be had locally and no tapered leaders, so I did what the others did. I bought six-foot level leaders with dropper loops and dry flies with six-inch snells attached. By this time I was the possessor of equipment of sorts, and I also had acquired some degree of expertise from my tutor.

It was springtime, and that meant two things to me: trout and baseball. Glory be, the two did not conflict. I got in uniform promptly, got out on the field to be the first to pitch batting practice, went to the showers early, then headed across the Delaware River for the Musconetcong River.

The first Musconetcong trip was a very big day in my young life. The site of my adventure was directly below a dam not far from the road to New York. The trout were acting in a manner Mr. Rupp referred to as "jumping." My Royal Coachman came down over the location of a busy fish. There was a slurp, a splash, a flash, and when I came up with the rod tip, the resistance which it met was electrifying. That skinny, pale, seven-inch brookie was the first trout I caught on a dry fly and no doubt my first hatchery-reared fish, a tremendous fish.

At the conclusion of the college year, I returned to the scene of my boyhood worming, little Cedar Run. What had been a twenty-minute bike ride from home was now about a seven-minute ride by car. This is the same Cedar Run along which Mr. Rupp was raised. It was the same stream, too, where I caught my first brookie and, years later, my first brown trout. In due time I learned by comparison how truly wonderful this little limestoner actually was with its superb "sulphur fly" hatch and accompanying evening rise of trout. What my small Light Cahills did there was a delight to Mr. Rupp, and of course, to me.

But now we were dealing with something different: two kinds of trout, the native brookies and the imported browns that averaged twice the size of the natives. The story of how the immigrant arrived is a good one.

Gus Steinmetz, an avid wet fly fisherman, was both news hawk and political speechwriter. One day in the spring of 1924 he received a call and the voice at the other end of the line said, "I am Herbert Hoover. I want you to take me trout fishing." Gus, believing it was a practical joker pulling his leg, promptly replied, "How are you, Herbie? I have been expecting your call." Well, it was the President, and Gus had been suggested as the one to take him fly fishing in the Harrisburg area. The two arranged an agreeable time, and Gus planned to take the President to Cedar Run.

As the time approached the grillie became apprehensive.

Maybe his charge was not slick enough to catch these smart fish? He pushed the panic button. An S.O.S. to the right man in the Department of Interior went something like this. "The big boss is going fishing with me next week. Send in catchable trout." The pump was primed with a truckload of buckets containing eight hundred "Loch Leven brown trout."

As it turned out, pressing business made the trip impossible, and Gus and the President never fished together, but southeastern Pennsylvania and the Yellow Breeches Creek watershed received its introductory stocking of brown trout.

A half-dozen years later we were dealing with the combination of brook and brown trout in Cedar Run. Mr. Rupp decided that the imports were every bit as interesting as the native brookies and twice as big. His crowning achievement was a four-pounder on his Light Cahill.

Just in time for the 1930 trout season, a book was published with the title, *Taking Trout with the Dry Fly* by Samuel G. Camp. The author sold his readers on the abomination of drag and made "drag" a dirty word. To overcome it he advised, "At the completion of the forward cast hold the rod motionless for a moment until the fly, floating down, has created more or less slack line, in accordance with the character of the water over which the cast has been made."

In the decades which followed I fished most of the evenings during the open season and came to appreciate and love the powerful limestone spring streams of the beautiful Cumberland Valley. Plans to live alongside one ultimately materialized.

In 1944 Vince Marinaro and I became fast friends and frequent angling companions. Perhaps the fact that we thought alike was the strongest possible bond. Our game was to try to intercept the hatches and encounter evening rises. We became deeply involved with the dainty daytime feeding activity and with developing imitations of the terrestrial insects on which the trout fed. In effect we were playing two games with the trout, or perhaps it would be more accurate to report that the trout were playing two games with us. Together we became involved in conservation matters, always, it seemed, losing the battles but in reality winning the war with the indirect help of Rachel Carson.

Since the late 1920's the ranks of fly fishermen and specifically fly fishermen who fish for trout have swelled into a closely knit army. We have the organizations of Trout Unlimited and the Federation of Fly Fishermen, plus literature the like of which no other sport can boast. The wonderful equipment and techniques now seen on trout streams and salmon rivers is matched only by the increased number of casters.

My trail has led through fifty seasons and it has passed through many waters. Frequently there has been the fly rod for company plus numerous fine companions and great fellowship. I am grateful that I have lived at the time when equipment was refined, when introduced brown trout created their own native populations and when restricted killing became the vogue in regulated areas. This period has been the foundation for dry-fly fishing in America. It is saddening, however, to see my beloved streams—Cedar Run, Big Spring and the Letort—suffer unnecessary deterioration from an instrument they call "progress."

# The Mangrove Pocket

CHARLES WATERMAN



The unnamed bay is several miles from the open Gulf of Mexico, and it is a long way from a boat dock. A few years ago it was seldom visited by fishermen, and hardly any of those who crossed it knew of the deep pocket near the center where big tarpon found a little added warmth on chilly days. In summer the deep pocket is a little cooler than surrounding shallows.

It is brackish water, its salinity varying with the rainfall in the sawgrass Everglades only a little farther inland, and the entire bay is ringed by mangroves with spider-leg roots reaching for mud and water. There is tidal movement, but it is so far from the Gulf that the rise and fall is slight, and when there are heavy rains inland the water sometimes moves outward all day and becomes quite fresh. It is black water, stained by vegetation, and the snook living along the shore have dark olive backs, very different from the silvery fish of the offshore islands. Tarpon of the nameless bay have dark backs although their sides have the gleam of polished steel plates, and when a fish rolls lazily on a calm day the sun shows brassy iridescence where the dark back grades into the gleaming side.

My old friend, the guide, had known about the fish and the deep pocket for a long time, and I do not know how he found them. Perhaps he happened to see a long, glistening back from a distance as one of the fish rolled. Perhaps he had felt the distinctive thumps as his outboard crossed above them, and he may have heard or seen a booming strike, but he knew the fish were living there, even at times when moving tarpon were scarce along the coast. For years hardly any anglers fished for them, for few fishermen associate the larger fish with the back country. For that matter, my friend the guide was secretive about the spot, and the only anglers he brought there were those who either could not find their way back to the fish or who lived a long way off and would have no desire to return in other company.

The deep hole was only about eight or nine feet deep, varying somewhat with the tides, but the surrounding waters were only four or five feet deep, and the bottom depression was thus very important. At times it would attract big jack crevalle, and there were nearly always gafftopsail catfish there, despised by bait fishermen and sometimes willing to strike a plug or fly. Although the borders of the bay were very good snook fishing, the snook were never caught over the deep area. Because several tidal streams merged in the area, there were frequent visits by traveling fish. At times there were sizable schools of channel bass (known in that area as redfish) along the shorelines. Other temporary visitors were porpoises and sharks, and now and then a fisherman could see the enormous shadow of a sawfish, as long as his boat, proceeding methodically in its weaving gait.

The tarpon did not spend all their time in the deeper hole, and there were days when they rolled leisurely through small schools of baitfish at the mouth of a little creek at one end of the bay, making wide swirls dotted by the spatters of the frantic prey. It was quite different when they crashed angrily at schools of big mullet in more open water. The bang sometimes sounded like a large-caliber pistol, and sometimes it was a more booming sound that left a great ragged patch of foam.

And on days when the surface was glassy, the big fish sometimes hung so near the top that their fins showed above the water, and from a distance they would look like floating scraps of debris, possibly pieces of palmettos from farther upstream where the "boots" of the trees sometimes flaked away and drifted out to the gulf.

Sometimes the tarpon were in a shallow, muddy end of the bay, not far from the shore, and in no more than three feet of water. As a boat drifted very slowly toward them with gentle encouragement from careful oars or paddle, those fish appeared as indistinct shadows, and a fisherman would study a shadow and try to tell which was the head and which was the tail. Less observant anglers could take the long shadows for sunken logs and would swear when they suddenly left in storms of underwater mud, each stroke of a big tail making its separate boil, and the fish itself, no longer seen, moved swiftly ahead of its murky trail.

And later, when we made a really serious effort to catch big tarpon, we often cast blind as our boat drifted for some three-hundred yards across the bay's center and its deeper pocket, and we would sometimes see a darker shadow two or three feet down, a long cast ahead of our course, and our hands would be a little unsteady on casting reel or fly line as we measured the distance and looked nervously about to see if the gaff was there and ready. At such a time we would think of the capabilities of our companions and secretly plan the landing operation, even before our cast was made.

There was the time when I saw a shadow near shore, and I cast the streamer fly to what I thought must be the fish's head. This time I was right, and the streamer fly went a little ahead of the fish, sank briefly, and then came back past the fish's eyes. He lay as a loafing tarpon rests against the mud, his undershot jaw parallel to the bottom and his tail a little higher than his head, dead still as if asleep, but with big staring eyes that must have seen whatever happened within their range and certainly saw the long yellow streamer and its breathing red hackle as it passed within two feet. After the streamer had passed, the tail moved deliberately, a slow movement combined with a sucking action, and I swung upward with the rod to feel solid weight. The fish ran against the reel and then jumped repeatedly to stir a sea of mud. But it was a small fish, no more than thirty-five pounds, and we nosed it into a big landing net to remove the hook.

I used black bass tackle, except that the streamer was a little larger, and I was a snook fisherman although I had long been gleefully appreciative of small tarpon that appeared as an added attraction with their clattering leaps which occasionally ended in shoreline mangroves, and once or twice they had jumped into the boat itself. Then I decided I would like to land a big tarpon on a fly, and that bay, some fifty miles from Everglades City and the nearest boat landing, was the place to do it.

Even then the hundred-pound tarpon on a fly was not too much of a rarity. These fish were usually caught in the Florida Keys by specialists who had studied thick-walled glass fly rods, knew of mysterious knots and shock tippets, and had perfected the technique of bowing to the big fish's leap to save their tackle. But the techniques were almost unknown in the dark mangrove waters where the tarpon's jumps were exciting but where landing the fish had been unimportant. Now I wanted to catch one.

I went to Miami to learn how it was done, but most of the instruction was a little vague and occasionally contradictory. My bonefishing associates had never bothered with tarpon. Literature on the subject was devoted to drama rather than technique, and I already knew how a big tarpon looked in the air and how he rattled his gill covers. I assembled my tackle—a heavy glass rod built from section of surf stick (stiffer than necessary, but I didn't know that) and a fairly large-capacity bass and salmon reel with modest drag and of modest cost. I had backing of squidding line and a short leader tapered to the contest fisherman's twelve-pound test. My shock tippet was a ten-inch piece of leader wire. I had a large number of big streamers with sharp hooks and in combinations of red, white, and yellow.

I knew the fish were large enough, for big mangrove tarpon had been caught there for more than fifty years, usually with trolling rigs or with big mullet baits on the bottom attached to heavy boat rods. There were 150-pound and larger tarpon, and some heavy fish had been caught on flies as shown in Dimock's *Book of the Tarpon*, but that had been a long while ago. My friend, the guide, said it was time somebody began it again. He went with me several times to get me started, and after that I took an assortment of my friends to the bay, some of them kindly and tolerant, others hopeful of catching a big fish themselves—but none of them had ever caught a big tarpon on light tackle.

The trip would start at dawn because it was a two-hour run. The trip often began with fog on the water, and the tops of the mangrove trees seemed to float above it. At first I used a chart to find the series of creeks and tidal rivers broken by a series of bays, but after the first few days I remembered the channels of deep water, sometimes lined by menacing oyster bars and protruding mud banks at low tide, and I would sit and plan my attack with the howling outboard just behind me. The little aluminum skiff rode high in the water with its bottom vibrating as I crossed the ripples in the back-country bays. In the narrow creeks I idled nervously, eager to get going again. The propeller would occasionally bump underwater logs gently, but it was turning slowly so that no real damage was done.

Although the bay was filled with fish, I realize now that I must have been unlucky, for I lost a great many of them, not from leader breakage but simply because the hook came out. Part of the time I used big popping bugs, and although they produced horrendous strikes, the fish simply pushed them out of the way as they struck at them. I finally learned that a living thing that made as much noise as a stridently worked popper would normally be heavy enough that the fish could get it, no matter if his bow wake was an oceanic wave. The cork and balsa poppers simply bobbed away.

There was one streamer-hooked fish which simply kept going. It was not a particularly large tarpon, but it left in a straight line, greyhounding in a series of low, distance-getting leaps, and the leader snapped when the backing was gone. Someone was slow in getting the motor started. Then there was another small fish which began the same thing, and I yelled for power without a previous outboard-motor checkout with my companion, and he started it in gear, wide open (you had to know about that motor). I was thrown from the bow, and I landed on the back of my neck atop an array of gasoline tanks. Burning ashes from my pipe showered the flustered helmsman, but we landed that fish.

Somehow, all the fish over fifty pounds got away, and probably only part of it was luck. We must have made mistakes unlikely for more experienced big-fish seekers. Once we ran the intricate way home in a driving rainstorm and darkness after a friend had played a really big fish for hours, never certain just how much pressure he could apply. And the largest tarpon I believe I have ever seen took my fly close-in near the bow and ran the fourteen-foot length of the boat with the line sizzling up a roostertail on the surface to jump almost straight up near the stern. He seemed to hang there above us, black and silver, with an aura of showering drops and leaving a broad hole in the water. It could not possibly have been as large as it seemed, but by then we had seen many tarpon in the air.

Then I hooked a special fish much as I had hooked others and lost them, but by this time I was accepting their strikes with relative calmness. The fish made the slow turn that churned the surface, and when I felt the tug I had set hard, and the fish had come out twisting and clattering its gill covers to fall back with a boom. I still had him after he had done that half a dozen times. Then he made a long run, and my friend followed him skillfully with the boat at the proper distance while I recovered backing. When the fish made a run along the shoreline, (another fish had brushed the leader apart with mangrove roots) I somehow held him clear, and when he started down one of the little tidal rivers I strained at him and creaked my rod, and he came to an almost dead stop and swam back toward the deep pocket in the bay.

I had the fish on for almost an hour, and it suddenly dawned on me that I might land this one. I had watched apprehensively as the line-to-backing splice came in and out the tip guide, and then there was no longer need for backing. The thick fly line gathered bulkily on the reel, and I saw the fish plainly, circling the boat slowly and blindly at the end of his tether, coming to the surface now and then with a sighing sound. Then, there was my leader knot out of the water, and the fish was on his side for a moment. He righted himself again and went feebly downward only to be pulled back up by the insistent lifting of the big rod. In close now and in plain view, the fish could be led at my will, and after an hour of giving instantly obeyed instructions to my boatman, I heard him now ask how to gaff the fish. A small and athletic man, he stood with the little release gaff in his hand. He was a famous caster and bass fisherman, and he had never gaffed any fish in his life.

I told him to put the sharp gaff in the fish's jaw and pull up with the short, knotted rope.

"I'll stick him from inside his mouth," he said.

He knelt at the gunwale and I brought the tarpon past, its tail waving slowly; it veered away.

The little man with the gaff cursed gently.

"Bring him back," he said.

The fish came alongside again, and the man with the gaff was crouched and tense, but he did not move the hook. I almost told him to gaff the fish, but I said nothing.

"That is not right," the man said.

I brought the fish around once more, and it took time, for the tarpon had gone under the boat and had made a short run. This time the man said nothing, but stuck the little gaff in the tarpon's jaw and stood half erect, knees against the gunwale. His shoulders bunched and shook as the fish threshed.

"I will not let him go," he said.

It was not a prize tarpon, but it was not a small tarpon either, and it had been a long campaign. I looked around the bay and gradually worked out my bearings so that I could get back to the dock before dark. I did not come back to the bay for several years after that. In the meantime the deep pocket had been discovered and fished hard, and the tarpon had left.

On the way in that night my friend sat amidships with his back to the wind. He looked at me and grinned. Once he put his head back and laughed aloud. I heard it over the squall of the old motor.

# The Night of the Gytefisk*

ERNEST SCHWIEBERT



*Skree-jah!* the arctic terns screamed. *Skree-jah!*

The sun was still low on the northern horizon, and strangely bright at two in the morning. The ghillies finally decided to break for lunch along the river. No one fishes except in the twelve-hour twilight of the midnight sun. The boatman expertly worked the slender Karasjok riverboat ashore, and its

*Pronounced jet•tay•fisk.

graceful Viking-like prow crunched on the gravel. It was cool for July, and a light wind riffled the huge pool at Steinfossnakken. The two boatmen built a fire on the beach while I watched the midnight sun on the waterfalls that spill Yosemite-like from the Sautso escarpment, a thousand feet above the river. The cooking smells of bouillon and hot coffee drifted on the wind, and we listened to the thundering Gabofoss rapids a mile upstream.

*Skree-jah!* screamed the terns shrilly.

The birds were catching mayflies, hovering and fluttering on the wind, and then dropping like an osprey to catch a hatching dun with a rapier-quick thrust of their beaks. Dark, red-finned grayling were working softly to the hatch in the shallows. The grayling averaged two pounds, but we were after bigger game. My three salmon lay gleaming in the boat, placed crosswise to ballast its slender hull. The best fish had been taken at Mostajokka, bright with sea-lice and a muscular thirty-three pounds. The smallest of the three went twenty-one, less than average for the river, and when it cartwheeled awkwardly at the end of its first long run, the riverkeeper had laughed and called it a grilse.

The sandwiches and hot soup warmed our bodies, and we finished our coffee, watching the river. Two river Lapps went past in the mail boat on their way to the Upper Sautso Camp. We were in no hurry now, with three fine salmon in the boat, even though we would fish another two hours before reaching the middle camp at Sandia.

It had been built in 1873 for the Duke of Roxburghe, its simple log frame virtually unchanged in a full century. It was my first night at Sandia, and in the morning, the mail boat was scheduled to carry me upriver to Sautso.

*Skree-jah!* the terns screamed.

The river begins in the snow-melt plateaus and escarpments of the Finnmarksvidda, two hundred miles above the Polar Circle in arctic Norway. The granite outcroppings bear the wounds and grinding scars of the ice-age glaciers that shaped them, leaving a vast wilderness pockmarked with dark tea-colored lakes.

The source of the river gathers in a series of potholes in the tundra barrens below Kautokeino, the village that is considered the capital of Lapland. Its surrounding highlands shelter a number of Lapp encampments, with their pyramidal log roofs and conical turf-cabins and storehouses on slender stilts. These are the permanent settlements where the Lapp herdsmen winter with their reindeer flocks and migrate with them in the spring, carrying their deerskin pole-shelters along on the trek. There is both humor and sadness in the coppery faces, wrinkled deeply with the fierce weather of those latitudes—it is a vanishing tribal way of life, like the world of the Eskimoes in its terrible arctic isolation.

The river rises in caribou-moss seepages in the treeless plateau, finally spilling into its deeply eroded valley about fifty miles north of Kautokeino. Its first twenty miles are locked in impenetrable gorges, filled with the lacework of countless waterfalls. There are salmon there too, spawning in a wilderness of impassable cliffs and rapids, but below its headwater canyons its character changes.

Its watercourse is a symphony in three movements: below the first tumbling chutes where the river escapes the gorge, its moods are almost pastoral, flowing into the mile-long mirror of smooth water below the Sautso Camp. Such *pianissimo* passages end in the wild cacophony of the Gabofoss rapids, where the river drops almost eighty feet in a quarter mile. Downstream from its portage, the river gathers in the amphitheater-sized Steinfossnakken, and its Sandia beats begin. These middle pools are a series of stairsteps, flowing swift and smooth into a brief rapids, and then swelling and spreading into another pool. The Sandia mileage ends in the moss-walled gorge above Battagorski, where the current fights its way through cabin-sized rocks—here are the clamor of brass and the thundering rhythms of kettledrums and cymbals. The river has claimed many lives in these rapids.

Its forests are denser now, thriving in the sheltered valley floor below the Battagorski water. There is a magnificent salmon pool there, deep and silken-smooth above great boulders in its chocolate depths, still flecked with foam from the rapids. It marks the top of the classic Jøraholmen beats, which wind in a sweeping series of pools—passages for strings and French horns and woodwinds—as they reach the farmstead clearings and villages above the sea.

The estuary is unimpressive, its currents shallow and spreading in a series of sandbar channels until they reach the fjord itself, a hundred miles below Hammarfest and the North

Cape. Bossekop is a brightly-painted fishing village at its mouth, its cheerful houses scattered on the hillsides. It was not always peaceful, because the fjord sheltered German pocket-battleships thirty-odd years ago during the bitter convoy battles that took place between Iceland and Murmansk.

The river has been fished and loved since the Duke of Roxburghe visited the fjord on his yacht in 1863, and discovered it was filled with huge salmon eager for his flies. Roxburghe and the Duke of Westminster, famed for both fishing and his liaisons with the late Coco Chanel, shared its fishing in the half-century before the Second World War. Roxburghe built the middle and upper camps in Victorian times, but in those early years they made their headquarters on the yacht moored off Bossekop. During the peak of the salmon run, parties poled and portaged upriver to the Sautso beats—fishing back to the luxury of the yacht at the pace of the current, and stopping in the several rough camps en route.

It has been fished in modern times by a whole parade of celebrated anglers. The late Duke of Windsor and his cantankerous equerry, the Earl of Dudley, were regulars a half-century ago. Death-duties and other shifts in the spectrum of British sovereignty on the river at mid-century, and anglers like Admiral MacDonald, Tony Pulitzer, Seward Johnson, Anderson Fowler, Ted Benzinger, Roger Gailliard, Sampson Field, Peter Pleydell-Bouverie, Clare de Bergh, Tom Lenk, Peter Kriendler, Cornelius Ryan, Edward Litchfield, Robert Goelet, Charles Ritz and Admiral Read—who successfully flew the NC-4 across the Atlantic long before Lindbergh—all became regulars over the past twenty-five years.

The Duke and Dutchess of Roxburghe still fish the river together each summer, and although its sport has declined seriously with deep-water netting of the salmon off northern Europe, it still remains perhaps the finest Atlantic salmon river on earth.

Its fishing history is unique. Twice in the past century, it surrendered more than thirty salmon to one angler in a single night. Both Roxburghe and Westminster accomplished that feat, taking fish that averaged almost twenty-six pounds. Sampson Field holds the modern record with seventeen fish in a: single night from the storied Gargia water—all taken with flies and averaging just under thirty pounds.

The river is the legendary Alta.

Charles Ritz records its fame in his classic *A Flyfisher's Life,* and has been heard singing its praises from the storied bar of his equally famous hotel in the Place Vendôme in Paris, to the quiet colonial-paneled quarters of the Angler's Club of New York below Wall Street.

*It is simply unique!* Ritz insists with excited gestures and staccato speeches. *There are no mountains except the Himalayas, no oceans like the Pacific, no fish like the Atlantic salmon—and only one Alta!*

Charles Ritz is right. Like a rock-climber who remains untested without attempting Dhaulagiri or Annapurna in Nepal, and the big-game hunter who has not stalked the Serengeti in Africa, the salmon fisherman dreams of fishing the Alta. Although its fishing on the Jøraholmen water had surrendered a half-dozen fish over twenty pounds in my two brief visits to the river, its sense of history and a brace of forty-pound salmon killed by the Duchess of Roxburghe and Peter Pleydell-Bouvarie, had haunted me for years.

It was the river that literally filled my dreams. *Valhalla!* Ritz insists. *It's Valhalla and once you have tasted it, nothing is the same!*

My first night at Sandia came about by accident. There was a fisherman who became ill there and had been taken downriver. Because I had arrived a day early from some poor fishing on the Reisa, the riverkeeper sent me upriver on the mail boat to fish out the sick man's last day. It was not so much a day of fishing for me, as the salmon I might catch belonged to the farmers who own the fishing rights and were worth considerable money. Although I felt a little like a trawler with my slender Garrison, we contributed ten salmon averaging twenty-three pounds to the river owners that first full night of fishing at Sandia.

The boatmen arrived after lunch to carry me upstream with the mail to Sautso, and we traveled through the Ronga and Mostajokka to the foot of the portage in the sprawling Steinfossnakken. We changed boats there, and the boatmen carried my heavy equipment on a pole to the lip of the Gabofoss above, while I carried my tackle and a duffle of fishing clothes and fly-tying gear over the boulder-strewn trail. The Gabofoss rapids thundered through its rocky course, blotting out all thought and other sound, and finally we reached the tail-shallows of the Sautso stillwater.

We spooked a huge salmon lying just off our second boat-mooring, and its bow-wave disturbed the rocky shallows of the lake. The boatmen stood looking at the chocolate-colored escarpments.

*Sautso is a paradise!* said the old boatman in Norwegian.

Finally, they loaded my gear in the second Karasjok boat and we started upriver toward the Sautso camp, crossing the smooth water of the river between Gabofoss and Sirpinakken.

The cabin at Sautso is simple and rough. It was built by the Duke of Roxburghe not long after the American Civil War. There is a simple sitting-room with log walls, two bedrooms with rudimentary baths, the kitchen and quarters for a cook and a serving girl. The ghillies sleep in a turf-cabin near the river. The sitting-room wall had the pale pencil tracing of a fifty-nine-pound salmon killed by Admiral Read at the Steinfossnakken on a huge Hairwing Abbey, and I reverently retraced its muscular outlines on the wainscoating with a brush dipped in Chinese ink.

Anglers with a sense of tradition owe something to posterity.

The afternoon sun was still bright when the cook informed me solemnly that dinner was scheduled for seven o'clock. Fishing would begin at eight. The black curtains shut out most of the afternoon light, but I slept fitfully, dreaming of the Sautso beat and its giant salmon. It was a setting worthy of my moment of truth, and sleep was difficult.

The dice-cup used to start the week awarded me the upper river from the Toppen, where the Alta escapes its impenetrable gorge, to the famous Dormenin, one of the few wadable pools on the Alta.

We traveled upriver just after supper, portaging the Karasjok boat around the Svartfossen rapids and the wild chutes at Bolvero and Jagorski. Toppen was above, flowing smooth and still in the last reaches of the gorge. The ghillies worked the boat cautiously up the smooth surface and stopped for a pipeful of tobacco in the narrows above the trail.

*We must rest the fish,* they explained in Norwegian. *Give the salmon time to forget us.*

Finally we began fishing.

It was a roll-casting place with a sheer basalt wall behind the boat, and I had to loop the fly about thirty-five feet against the opposite rocks. The old boatman rowed patiently with the smooth current, letting his skiff drop about two feet downstream for each succeeding cast. His was precise work, requiring discipline and strength and a knowledge of the river.

I worked ten casts along the rocks, locking the line under my index finger with the rod-tip low, following the swing when the line came around toward the stern. I lifted the rod to raise it over the ghillie there, and then let it hang a few seconds downstream to the left of the boat. Sometimes a fish following the fly-swing will take when the fly stops. Sometimes one will take as it starts moving again and will follow the fly across the current and hang under it, circling its position, and take when the fisherman starts a short, upstream retrieve toward his boat.

Salmon fishing is discipline and patience on a big river like the Alta. One must cover its half-mile riffles with a series of concentric fly-swings. The mind can drift and daydream with the rhythm of the oarlocks and the casting: and suddenly there was a huge swirl behind the swinging fly.

*Laks!* said the boatman softly.

The fish had come after the fly-swing without taking it, and we quickly repeated the cast.

*He's coming again!* the ghillie whispered.

There was literally a bow-wave, bulging under the smooth current. Sometimes you can force a take by varying the swing, and this time I slowed the teasing rhythm of the rod tip and stripped about six inches of line toward the bellying fly. It slowed the swing, forcing the following salmon to make a choice: overrun the fly and turn back, or take it.

This one hesitated a millisecond and took. The rod snapped down as the bellying line revealed its weight, and there was a wild tail-splash as it turned head-down and sounded.

Several times it threatened to leave Toppen, working deep into the shallows at the tail, but each time we forced it back into the deep water in the throat of the gorge. Finally, the boatman slipped out of the main currents, and I pumped the salmon close; the ghillie reached deftly with the gaff, wresting a fat thirty-pound henfish over the gunwale. He dispatched it with a sharp rap of the priest behind the ears and laid it gleaming across the thwarts of the boat.

*Det var findt!* he grinned.

We rested the pool again for a half hour and took a second

big salmon right at the lip of the rapids. below the broken quarter-mile downstream is the Jagotku chute, where the late Joe Brooks took a forty-pounder, and I killed a lively ten-kilo* fish there wading, as the boatmen wrested our skiff down the whitewater of the other channel.

Svartfossnakken was next, the sprawling pool where the river turned sharply and gathered speed in a dark, ink-colored slick at its tail. The Svartfoss rapids lay below, tumbling through a long, sickle-shaped curve at the base of the mountain. The boatmen hold their skiff expertly here in the gathering currents, stroking evenly and well, while the fisherman casts a lengthening line over the swift, foam-flecked shallows. We hooked a heavy fish there almost immediately, and the ghillies fought to maintain position while I forced the salmon. It did not work, and the fly came out. The ghillies saw that I was not unhappy, and we laughed together, resting the pool. We had three fish in the boat, and that was par on the Sautso beat.

We took a second fish from Svartfoss, and I walked downriver to Dormenin while the ghillies lowered the boat on the anchor line through the Svartfoss rapids. Dormenin is perhaps the best greased-line pool on the Sautso beat, and I changed reels to use a floating line. Twice I moved a fish at the head, but it refused to come again. Another rolled sullenly at the tail, where Dormenin eddies and slides into the Harstrommen stretch. It proved unproductive too, and we finally traveled downriver, having reached the bottom of our first night's beat.

*Fire fiskar!* the ghillie beamed.

It had been a four-fish night, and we were ahead of the three-fish par on this beat, so the boatmen were pleased. The morning was dark and overcast, and when we reached the camp at the Jotkajavrre tributary, the smooth expanse of Sautso was patterned with a misting rain.

*Stormy tomorrow night,* said the boatmen gloomily. *Tomorrow we fish Gabo and Velleniva.*

*They're good pools?* I asked.

*Excellent!* they said.

It was raining hard at four in the morning, the drops drumming on the roof-shingles, and it was getting lighter under

---

*One kilo is the equivalent of 2.2 pounds.

the heavily overcast skies. The maids brought us our supper (the days and nights being upside down on the Alta) and at six, after dressing several large Orange Blossoms on 3/0 doubles, I finally drew the black, bedroom curtains against the gathering daylight and fell asleep, listening to the rain.

It was afternoon when the young maid awakened me, but it was gloomy and dark. The overcast had lowered between the ragged escarpments that enclosed the valley, until it hung like an immense shroud a few hundred feet above the river. My breakfast of fried eggs and goat cheese and brislings was ready, and the ghillies waited unhappily in the kitchen.

It did not feel like a fishing night. *The barometer must have drained through the grass,* I said.

*Ja,* the boatmen agreed sourly.

We traveled upstream to the gravel-bar island at Dormenin and began fishing upper Harstrommen. The overcast was even lower, until scraps of mist drifted through the trees, and it was raining again. We shouldered into our ponchos unhappily, studying the sullen current. Its tea-color had turned milky, and the river was rising a little. The ghillie selected a fresh Orange Blossom, the pattern that had killed well the night before, and painstakingly knotted it to the nylon. Then we worked across the current and fished the sixty-yard pool carefully in spite of the rain and mist.

*Nothing!* I said when we had fished through the entire pool. *It's too gloomy tonight!*

*Perhaps it's a Gytefisk night,* they said.

*What's that?* I asked.

*There are nights when we catch almost nothing even on the Alta,* the ghillie in the stern explained, *but our name for a big cockfish that has spawned before and come back again is Gytefisk.*

*And some nights you catch a Gytefisk?*

*Ja,* said the boatman, *and they usually come on nights when nothing else will take the fly!*

*Let's pray for a Gytefisk night,* I said.

*Ja,* they smiled.

The current seemed even more discolored. It called for a pale fly the fish could easily see, and I studied my boxes. There was a bright yellow-hackled Torrish that Clare de Burgh had given me at lunch with Charles Woodman in Oslo. They had been fishing a week earlier with Seward Johnson, Anderson

Fowler and Carter Nicholas on the Jøraholmen beat at Alta, and Clare had been high rod with thirty-seven salmon. She had also killed a superb cockfish of fifty-seven pounds.

*Every bloody one on the Torrish!* She laughed. *You take my last one and try it!* it lay glittering on the tablecloth.

*I'll enshrine it and make copies!* I said.

It looked enticing in the box. There had been no time to copy it, but its bright hackles and glittering tinsel seemed perfect. The ghillie seemed skeptical, but he took the Torrish and knotted it to the tippet. It looked good working in the current beside the boat.

It was raining harder when we reached the lower Harstrommen. It is a heavy, hundred-yard reach of water named for its strong currents. The boatman expertly maneuvered the longboat into position at the head of the pool, and we began fishing it methodically.

*Good place?* I asked in Norwegian.

*Ja,* they shook their heads. *We do not catch many salmon here—but usually big ones.*

*Good place for Gytefisk?* I suggested.

*Perhaps,* they smiled.

It was almost prophetic. The line worked out into the gathering darkness and dropped the fly sixty-five feet across the current tongue. I lowered the rod and let the fly settle deep into its bellying swing; suddenly there was a sullen pull that stopped its teasing rhythm. The line throbbed with both the fish and the current, and I sat down to fight it. The salmon seemed unusually strong, but it was too early to tell, feeling its weight and power alone in such currents.

*Gytefisk?* I smiled nervously.

The boatmen said nothing, working the oars and watching the throbbing, almost sullen movements of the rod. They seemed unusually concerned at the tenor of the fight, and suddenly I understood why. The river exploded slightly above the boat, and an immense, sow-sized fish cartwheeled awkwardly, landing with a gargantuan splash.

*My God!* I thought wildly.

The fish burst halfway out of the river a minute later, broaching like a whale and falling again heavily.

*Thirty kilos!* guessed the ghillie.

*Ja!* the boatmen agreed.

Both men were talking excitedly, more excited than I had seen them on the night before, and we began the grim business of fighting such a fish in heavy water on a light fly-rod. It was hard work.

The salmon hung angrily for several minutes, and then turned almost majestically downstream, gathering speed in the tumbling currents below the boat. Its strength seemed to ignore any pressure we could exert, and it took a hundred yards of backing with almost ridiculous ease. Then it stopped ponderously. The boatmen used those precious minutes to maneuver for better position, and we crossed the Harstrommen to get our longboat into the backwater shallows a little below the fish. It shook its head slowly and sourly at midstream.

I had just begun to pump-and-reel saltwater style, holding the rod in a modified tarpon lock, when the salmon started slowly out of the pool. There was nothing we could do, and it simply shouldered us aside, gathering speed as it reached the swift rapids.

*Thirty kilos is over sixty-five pounds,* I kept thinking wildly. *Sixty-five pounds!*

The backing dwindled dangerously on the spool, and the boatmen worked desperately to follow, rowing and sometimes poling to keep both the line and the longboat free of the rocks. It was a wild, half-mile trip with no control over the salmon.

It easily fought us through several pools, forcing us another mile through Battanielo and Banas and the smooth, swelling currents of Sirpinakken. More white water lay below, but it was less tumbling and broken, and we came through with the fish still hooked. The fight went better in the lake-sized shallows just above the Sautso camp.

The huge salmon porpoised weakly, circling fifty yards out. It seemed beaten, and now the rod-pressure could stop its attempted runs. Finally, it surrendered to my saltwater lock, and came grudgingly out of the heavy currents into the pondlike Jotka backwater.

The fly-line was back on the reel now, its dark green turns covering the pale, Dacron backing line. We forced the huge salmon closer and closer until the leader was showing above the water. The salmon rolled almost under the boat, and we gasped at its size.

*Thirty kilos,* the ghillies whispered in awe.

The salmon bolted weakly, stripping out fifteen yards of line, but I turned it slowly back to the boat. The ghillie moved the gaff soundlessly into position, waiting like a heron. The fish floundered and surfaced, rolling weakly and working its gills, and it was almost in reach of the gaff when it gasped, and the fly came free.

*Damn!* I shouted unhappily.

The ghillie cursed and threw the gaff angrily into the shallows. The boatman hung on his oars and stared as the great fish gathered its strength and turned into deeper water, pushing a bow-wave like a half-submerged submarine. Alta ghillies are usually so taciturn that such an emotional performance startled me, and I reeled in trying not to laugh.

Later, the riverkeeper explained that the Alta record is a sixty-pound cockfish killed by the Earl of Dudley during the time he served as equerry to the late Duke of Windsor. Dudley was so unpopular for his treatment of the ghillies that he is the only foreign angler who ever fell into the Alta, having belly-flopped over a gunwale into the Kirkaplassen shallows. The riverkeeper and his boatmen only smile when asked about the story that Dudley's baptism was a planned retribution, executed with a deft shift of balance in the stern of a Karasjok longboat.

*The Earl of Dudley was a difficult man,* said the riverkeeper. *We have watched dukes and princes and kings all our lives—and we knew an equerry was only a ghillie in the world of palaces.*

He explained that my boatmen had both wanted to share in a new record for the Alta, and to displace the Earl of Dudley as its holder. Both ghillies had been certain the huge cockfish was over sixty pounds.

The fish had carried us down several pools, through a good two miles of river, and the unsuccessful fight had gone an hour and forty minutes. We gathered ourselves with great disappointment, knowing we had lost the chance of a lifetime. It started to rain again, and the gloomy overcast hung fifty feet off the river. The night held little promise.

*Let's try another place,* I sighed.

Goddanienii lies just below the camp, where the foamy current works two hundred yards along the steep toe-faces of the Steinfjeldet mountain. It eddies past a rockfall into the similar current called Goddanielo. We fished through both places twice because they had been extremely productive the week before, but there was only a dark, two-pound, breakfast grayling.

The Sautso lake is filled with big grayling here, but even they were not dimpling for the tiny *Anisomera* midges that night. It was a discouraging sign when even the grayling were dour.

*The river seems dead,* I said and shook my head unhappily. *Not even a rise of grayling tonight.*

*Let's fish Velliniva,* suggested the ghillie.

*Good pool?* I asked.

*It's the best pool at Sautso,* he smiled. *We should move something there, even tonight.*

*Let's go,* I said.

Velliniva is a beautiful, hourglass-shaped narrows in the Sautso lake. It was strangely still that night, and the overcast had lifted slightly. There are truck-sized boulders in the river, and a ledge crosses it in a series of shallows at the tail of the pool. It is the last place before the gathering currents above Gabofoss rapids, the impassable reach of water that divides the Sandia and Sautso beats. Gabofoss is a holding-lie I never liked, as it seemed dangerous to row steadily only a cast-length away from certain death. The ghillies often row simultaneously there, watching the lip of the rapids warily to judge the remaining margin of safety.

We fished through both places without moving a salmon. It was getting lighter now and my watch read three o'clock. We started slowly upriver, discouraged with both the weather and our luck, and as we crossed its still currents its mood seemed imperceptibly changed.

*Let's try Velliniva again,* I suggested.

The boatman smiled. *We always try Velliniva on our way home,* he explained. *It's our ritual.*

It was perfectly still, and the night turned strangely warm. Flies were hatching now, and the arctic terns appeared, capturing the tiny insects in midflight. The smooth current seemed strangely alive while we rested Velliniva to let the salmon forget our passing boat.

Twenty minutes passed. *Let's fish,* they said.

The fly-swing stopped on the third cast, and the still current erupted with a giant fish. *It's not like the fish we lost,* I shouted, *but it's big!*

*Twenty kilos,* said the ghillie softly.

The fight went well. I held the fish away from the boulders deep in the pool and worked it out of the main holding-lie. It did not jump again, and wasted its strength running upriver against the bellying line. The boatman gaffed it cleanly in twenty minutes.

*Just under twenty kilos,* he said.

It was a fine cockfish, just beginning to lose its polished, sea-armored coloring with the first bronzish cast of spawning. It did weigh just under twenty kilos, pulling my Chatillon scale to the forty-three-pound mark. The ghillies bled the fish and laid it across the boat. It seemed like a perfect ending, and I started to take down my gear.

*Nei!* the ghillie shook his head. *We must fish the pool again with such a big Gytefisk taking!*

*Fine,* I laughed.

Fifty yards below the lie where the first salmon had taken, the silken currents are perceptibly faster, and the boatman increased his rhythms to lower us more slowly down the current. It made us cover the water with more closely spaced casts, and I realized they considered it the hot-spot of the entire pool. The terns were still working the surface of the river, and the morning sun turned the overcast pinkish gray. Its warmth was burning through the darkness.

Six casts fished out before there was an immense swirl, showing a guillotine-sized tail and a silvery flank that caught the morning light. The line tightened with a wrenching sprain, and then the salmon jumped, the bright-yellow Torrish clearly visible in its jaws.

*Good lord!* I shouted happily. *It's huge!*

It was another big cockfish, pinwheeling full length from the river and landing with a shattering splash that disturbed the entire pool.

*Skree-jah!* screamed the terns.

The fish jumped again, falling belly down like a giant marlin, and stripped a hundred yards of backing in a sullen run up the lake. We followed it grudgingly to recover line and hold our angle on the fish, but it turned with sudden, explosive power and bulldogged angrily past the boat. The reel shrieked and protested as the salmon gathered speed, and the pale backing blurred through the guides.

We turned the boat to follow, hoping the line would not foul in the bottom ledges deep in the belly of the pool. The fish did not sound there, and our luck held. It threshed powerfully in the swift tail-currents and was over the chutes into the still water downstream.

The fish had traveled a current-tongue too risky for our long boat, and we followed down a closer channel. While we negotiated it safely, the fish achieved a few minutes of slack. It fouled the backing on a shoal of stones. Its strength was largely spent, and unlike the monster salmon at the beginning of the night, our luck still held. The boatman worked carefully around the shoal while the ghillie in the stern plunged his boat-pole deep in the river, working the foul line free.

The huge salmon was still hooked. It rolled weakly in the still currents now, and I pumped it close until the gaff went home. Its muscled bulk came threshing in over the side, and when a blow with the priest stilled its struggling, we saw it was even bigger than the fish that lay gleaming in the boat. It scaled forty-six pounds, and I stood looking at them in disbelief, and when we took a third fish of thirty-nine pounds it seemed a strange anticlimax. When the last salmon was boated, the ghillie reverently examined the Torrish.

Its yellow hackles were matted and worn, its hairwing ragged and thinning badly. Two long spirals of loose tinsel wound free of the body; the dark working silk showed the hook.

The ghillie cut it from the leader, held it high in the growing early morning light and threw it far into the pool.

*It belongs to the river now,* he said.

The boatman bled the fish expertly. *It's been a strange night,* I said. *Losing a monster, and boating three salmon like these!*

*It was a night of the Gytefisk,* they smiled.

# The Crossing of the Caribou

DANA S. LAMB



You didn't drive or fly to Maine when I was young; you took the train. As the engine gathered speed you saw the outer city's lights come on and when you walked across the lurching platform to the dining car you caught the soft, warm smell of tar.

Now, more than likely, seated by the window waiting for your order of lamb chops in ruffled paper pants, Maine sweet potatoes and green corn, a bluff and sun-tanned stranger took the seat across the table and began to talk.

Perhaps he'd say, "I heard you say you didn't want that Kennebec, boiled salmon; said you'd catch your own next week. You must be heading for my state."

"Yes sir, I'm headed up to Maine."

"I'm traveling down to Maine myself," he'd say. "That's what I call my stampin' ground. But I'd consider this a mite too late; we mostly quit our salmon fishing in the Bangor Pool the end of June."

Then you might tell him you were going after landlocks near Fort Kent and say that some of them were pretty big—larger than some sea-run fish.

And possibly he'd say he knew that that was true; some Portland friends of his had taken ten-pound landlocks in Sebago Lake. But he, himself, preferred to fish a river than a lake.

"That's why I take my holiday this time of year," I'd say. "I like to fly-fish in the thoroughfares instead of trolling in the lakes. Those landlocked salmon leave deep water in the fall; you find them in the streams between the lakes. I guess they want to have their spawning beds prepared a month or two before the winter closes in."

The train now shudders to a stop; the waiter brings the ice cream and the macaroons; I pay the bill. The stranger smiles and says: "Penobscot's had its finest season yet this year; it might just be the same up by the border. I hope it is; I wish you luck."

Murmuring a word of thanks, I walk on back—the scent of marshes and low tide is strong—to where my lower bunk is ready for my dreams. The train rolls onward in the night, racing with September's orange moon. I see it—always even—slicing silently through banks of clouds; I am happy, healthy and content, and need no opiate to make me sleep.

That's about the way it was in 1921.

Next morning in the sleeping car, the porter helped those people who were bound for Rangeley and its sister lakes to shift their rods and duffle to another train. Augusta took its toll of Belgrade fishermen with reservations at the Liar's Paradise. Bangor was the stopping place where some of us bade goodbye to the businessmen, the folks who came to close their summer homes on Mount Desert or salmon anglers headed for the Miramichi. Here I turned off for Osprey Lake.

My car was hitched up now to ancient shopworn mates behind a locomotive short on paint. But if equipment wasn't all that one could wish, the service was. The trainmen—it was difficult to tell just who was which—were calm and kind. Each waistcoat pocketed a fat gold watch with massive chain, each wallet in a man's blue jacket held encyclopedic information on New England's railroad trains, and every well-fed fellow had a heart made glad by helping out his fellow man.

"Keep a close watch out this window now; we're coming to a mighty likely place to see a moose," one said.

Another said: "I think you'd be right smart to get a coat or sweater from your bag before we get much further on. If you're headin' in for Marchand's camp, I guess you'll wish you had on something warm the time you get across the lake to Marchand's dock."

Osprey Lake, the only village on the wooded shores of Osprey Lake, was so all-fired starved for entertainment that its residents—except the folks too sick or hurt to walk—turned out to watch the coming of the day's one railroad train. Among them, Philippe Pluard, alerted by employers at the big lake's only sportsman's camp, was quick to greet the single passenger to leave the train.

"I am Philippe Pluard, who will be your guide," he said. "I put your baggage in the boat, and then I go and get the mail. When it is ready we will go to camp."

Osprey is a major unit in Aroostook County's Rushing River Chain of Lakes. From its low, surrounding hills the forests march down to the water's edge, endless ranks of evergreens without a gap for farmhouse or for summer camp. Some years before the time of which I write, young salmon of a migratory strain were introduced and outlets of the lower lakes were wired off so fish could not escape downstream. Ultimate return from their traditional feeding places in the sea had long been blocked by unenlightened industry. Fortunately, the system's larger lakes served well as little inland oceans, providing smelts and other sustenance as well as absence of extremes in water temperatures. From the safety and the comfort of their depths the fish ran up or down connecting streams; down in spring to feed on spawning smelt; and up in the fall, themselves to reproduce. While each year thousands fished the Beaverkill for trout, and hundreds sought the salmon in the Restigouche and the Miramichi, only a corporal's guard competed for these lovely native fish of Maine.

Eagerly I looked back from the sunset toward the night; toward camp and toward next morning on the thoroughfare.

On the dock our host stood in the dusk. The gentle, well-loved Pierre Marchand with mellow, low-pitched voice called out a greeting and my name. With well-tied knots the boat was soon secured against the weathered float's protected landward side; the men transferred my baggage to a cabin on the rocks. Philippe turned up the lamps, put fresh wood on the fire and brought a pail of water from the spring while Pierre showed me the ropes.

"The path leads up the little hill to where we eat," he said. "You'll hear the bell and see the lanterns in the windows of the lodge. The rods we always keep inside the screen to protect the handles from the porcupines. That running water that you hear is coming from a big lake up above us here, Round Lake. It was beside these camps of ours the caribou would cross the river every year; my father saw them swim across the year he died. That was many years ago; they say they never crossed again, but just this season one dark night when I was here alone in camp I thought I saw the caribou go by. The fog was thick, there was no moon; I can't be sure. I'll leave you for a little while and see you later at the lodge."

Next morning, off the nearby river's mouth, we took a turn or two with Philippe paddling in the stern, and Gray Ghost trolled behind, but I only caught a single, small-sized trout. I'd never heard of Theodore Gordon. Halford, Skues, Hewitt or La Branche but, all the same, this seemed a dull and unrewarding form of sport. With a Jock Scott and a Silver Gray we moved up to the Outlet Pool.

The Outlet Pool looked promising enough to make it fun to fish regardless of results. I cast at least a hundred times and let the current swing the flies around. The patient Pluard changed position, changed the flies, to no avail, and at last suggested that we go upstream, eat our luncheon in the clearing by the warden's shack at the outlet of Round Lake and fish up there that afternoon.

"Sounds to me a good idea," I said. "Let's go ashore and

get our slickers and our mackinaws in case the weather changes."

When we started out again and went a mile or so upstream, Philippe leaned on his pole and said, "M'sieur Marchand, he say he wish you luck. He say he sorry not to see you at the lodge last night; he had bad dizzy spell and he not feel so good. He say he like to take you out for fish one day and be your guide himself before the season close. He say he have good dream big salmon sleep at mouth of brook outside long gravel bar at outlet of Round Lake. He say sometime you fish close in with big Green Drake; he think you catch."

"Let's hope our good friend Pierre is well again when we get back to camp tonight," I said.

My guide stood thoughtful for a while, then crossed himself and leaned on his pole and pushed up through the fallen, floating, yellow hardwood leaves until we saw, a little way ahead, a wide expanse of ruffled blue, Round Lake. There he ran our craft ashore, unloaded pots and pans, tin plates, canned goods, the tableware and such beside the bench that served the warden as a restful watching post beside the pool. With his hunting knife he shredded kindling from a white-birch log, cut fodder for a fire with his little axe and, in ten minutes, served a first-rate woodsman's lunch at which the moose-birds were uninvited, rather pushy guests.

The warden, who had lunched at Campbell's camp some miles beyond the islands in Round Lake, came by and joined us in a cup of coffee and a chat before he left to spend the night at Osprey Lake. When he was out of sight we lay down on our blankets in the shade and slept. We woke up in the middle of the afternoon and both at once gave thought to Marchand's dream of salmon, big and eager for the Green Drake fly, where Round Lakes ice-cold brook ran in outside the gravel bar.

"Let's go out, Philippe," I said.

We did, and, as we left the inlet, I saw a bull moose with a rack of horns of trophy size feeding in the lily pads. We watched him tearing at the lily roots and heard the water dripping when he raised his head from nostrils which he turned toward us suspiciously. Cautiously we eased back in behind the bar and drifted through the pool and killed a three-pound fish and took it down to camp to give to Madame Marchand, who, we hoped, would cook it for Pierre. Then, happy and relaxed, I went to bed, ignoring dinner bells.

The wind lashed round the cabin all night long, the autumn rains came streaming down from raven skies. I awoke well rested and without the urge to get out on the river and to fight the elements. Philippe was standing by the stove. "M'sieur Marchand was taken to the hospital last afternoon," he said. "The warden, he don't like the way he look when he came by. He take him down."

"Philippe," I said, "you ask Madame if you can take her down today to see M'sieur. I know that he will be all right, but think, perhaps, she'd like to go."

"Merci," he said and went away.

For two days the storm kept up. I cowered in my cabin, read a book, fished fitfully the nearby outlet pool and slithered up the muddy path for cheerless meals.

After this the sun came back, likewise Philippe Pluard.

"M'sieur is better; he will be all right. He think we go, and Madame say so too, and spend two days, last days, where Round Lake run into top river pools. I have blankets and plenty food in my canoe. We sleep in warden's shack; he say OK. Your friend, Pierre, he think you get big salmon early in the morning at the brook. When you are ready, call; I wait for you."

All day I felt a kinship with Pluard upriver in the quiet woods. When evening came we talked about the caribou Pierre Marchand had thought he'd seen; about the dream Pierre had about the fish. Before we went to sleep Philippe had said: "You come again next year; you come back anytime and tell me, I will go with you. I will anytime go anywhere with you."

We ate our breakfast in the gray before the dawn and got out to the brook as it was getting light. No bull moose stood among the lily pads, no wind came down the lake to block the progress of my fly; my Green Drake landed where I wanted it to land. Just as the sun came out and warmed the air I saw the boil and felt a pull; a big fish ran along the bar and jumped. I saw a lovely silver fish, the biggest of its kind I'd ever seen. It leapt and diamonds flashed and sparkled in the sun; again, again and yet again. And then, at last it came to net, the miracle Pierre Marchand had seen in dreams.

"Let's go back down to camp; perhaps Pierre is back," I said. I found it difficult to speak.